Working with Girls and Young Women with an Autism Spectrum Condition

Working with Girls and Young Women with an Autism Spectrum Condition

A Practical Guide for Clinicians

FIONA FISHER BULLIVANT

Jessica Kingsley *Publishers*
London and Philadelphia

First published in 2018
by Jessica Kingsley Publishers
73 Collier Street
London N1 9BE, UK
and
400 Market Street, Suite 400
Philadelphia, PA 19106, USA

www.jkp.com

Library of Congress Cataloging in Publication Data
Names: Bullivant, Fiona Fisher, author.
Title: Working with girls and young women with Autism
Spectrum Condition : a practical guide for
   clinicians / Fiona Fisher Bullivant.
Other titles: Working with girls and young women with autism spectrum disorder
Description: London ; Philadelphia : Jessica Kingsley Publishers, 2018. |
   Includes bibliographical references.
Identifiers: LCCN 2017058734 | ISBN 9781785924200 (alk. paper)
Subjects: | MESH: Autism Spectrum Disorder | Professional-Patient Relations |
   Women--psychology | Personal Narratives
Classification: LCC RC553.A88 | NLM WS 350.8.P4 | DDC 616.85/8820082-
-dc23 LC record available at https://lccn.loc.gov/2017058734

British Library Cataloguing in Publication Data
A CIP catalogue record for this book is available from the British Library

ISBN 978 1 78592 420 0
eISBN 978 1 78450 784 8

Printed and bound in Great Britain

To Ann Hodges and your parents for sharing your lives in

For the Love of Ann

so I could read it at the age of eight and be inspired
to work with individuals with autism.

From misunderstood to Miss Understood...

Contents

Acknowledgements

Thank you to Darcey, Milly and Esther, as without you this book would not have been possible. Thank you for your honesty, your bravery, your resilience, your difference and your motivation, but most of all for being you. Thank you to your parents and your brothers and sisters for letting me into all of your hearts, minds and lives.

Thank you to my mum, Mavis, and my dad, Michael, two very important people in my life, for your love, encouragement, support and never ever faltering belief in me. To Michael, thank you for your love, being proud in what I do and for your continued support, and a special thank you for believing in me and encouraging me to do something I had been afraid of doing for so many years. To Jordan, for the mother–son chats, your love and your understanding of my work and its importance to me. Thank you for being so wonderfully you, you make me so proud every day. To all my friends and extended family who tolerate and embrace *my* differences.

To those many colleagues over many years who believed in me and my passion for my work. Thank you for challenging me, asking for my opinion, and for trusting me and encouraging me to share those opinions, knowledge and excitement.

Many thanks to my wonderful dogs (yep all four of them) for going on long walks with me, making me laugh, loving me unconditionally and keeping me emotionally well.

CONTRIBUTIONS

Thank you to Emelie Daniels, a Senior Mental Health Nurse Practitioner currently practising within the Child and Adolescent Mental Health Service (CAMHS), for her contribution. It's practitioners like Emelie who will help shape future services, as she has the insight and foresight that is needed to make clinical change.

Introduction

This book contains the voices and personal accounts of three young women with an autistic spectrum condition (ASC), alongside the experiences of their clinician, me, who joined them in part of their passage to their understanding, management and acceptance of themselves.

These three young women and their families will be sharing their experiences of services from their perspective: what worked well and what didn't.

The book will address the difficult but not unachievable challenge: how do we, services, clinicians and the wider community, understand, empower, and most importantly enable these intelligent, extraordinary young women to sustain a positive emotional state and a greater understanding and acceptance of themselves and their differences?

From my perspective as a clinician, the book is a compilation of my past and present experiences, reflections and future thoughts which have evolved from years of working with very complex individuals, girls and young women with often brilliant minds, mysterious souls and exceptional brains, but who often struggle with their identity, self-worth and general understanding of themselves – often wondering if they have a mental illness, often feeling disconnected and different but confused as to why, and often misunderstood and more concerningly missed and misdiagnosed.

This book will address and explore how best to match clinical expertise and experience with individualisation to address need and improve service provision. It will consider the therapeutic alliance and how individual need respects clinical adaptability and flexibility, as well as exploring a holistic approach to the care of the young person in order to inform appropriate assessment, care and services to support and enable the individual's wellbeing and resilience.

Clinical and professional skills and implementation of practice will be scrutinised in terms of advancements and adjustments needed in all areas of work in this field, and the book will aim to demonstrate the necessity for collaborative working with the individual and their families, including siblings and extended families. It will explore where we as clinicians and services go wrong and how we need to change and improve to offer a quality service, alongside celebrating expert and empathic practice and innovative ways of working and service developments. It will look at the complexities, challenges and achievements of clinical practice.

Throughout the book the young women's stories will weave through with examples of their experiences, their interactions with services and clinicians, their ups and downs, their setbacks and finally their successes. This will highlight the need for a culture change in clinical practice and service provision, so future assessments, diagnosis and ways of working are more timely, more helpful and more needs led.

My vision is that if we as clinicians and services are *brave, flexible and different*, then we can ask our young people to be brave and embrace their difference.

We expect the young people we work with to be courageous, to adapt to being different, but do we model these characteristics as clinicians?

CHAPTER 1

Why Girls and Young Women with an Autistic Spectrum Condition?

There is something about them, something different.
Something enigmatic and diverse.

This book is both a clinical and personal perspective of working with this captivating, magnificently complex, unique group of young women with ASCs. You cannot fail to be touched by their courage to seek an understanding of themselves, however hard and long that journey is for them.

I am a passionate, empathic clinician eager for my colleagues and other professionals to change and adapt their way of thinking and to shift the culture of how we understand and work with these intelligent but often episodically and sometimes chronically desperately distressed and confused young women.

This book is not about wanting or needing to change them as people or make them fit into a clinical box, it's about aspiring to enable and support them to understand themselves so they can be the best version of themselves they can and want to be.

It's not going to tell you anything amazingly new in terms of research or wonderfully diverse ways of working, but it will hopefully inspire you to be the best clinician you can be, and to be brave and flexible in your thinking and your practice.

My biggest hope is that it will motivate you to increase your skills and knowledge and awareness of ASCs within girls and young women and hopefully enthuse and spur you on to want to work in this particular clinical field with these remarkable individuals.

I am honoured to be travelling through the book with the following young women.

DARCEY, MILLY AND ESTHER

They have all experienced their own individual journeys with their families, starting off in generic health services then moving on to paediatric mental health services and diagnostic pathways. All three young women were unique in their symptoms and clinical presentation. All three had their own distinctive and charismatic way of expressing their emotions and thoughts, which warranted a personalised, individualised clinical approach and understanding. This is mine and their personal and clinical accounts of being involved in services and systems, and how the way services are delivered and managed impacts on individuals, clinicians and lives.

I came to work with these young women as a result of a chance appointment with another young woman almost ten years ago. I say 'chance', as she was not one of the children/young people I would usually see in my practice at that time as she had been referred into generic CAMHS, and I then worked with young people with ASC with an additional learning disability.

That changed for a while, however, (hence my chance meeting) as an insightful manager, Sarah, at the time supported and actively encouraged joint working across teams and across disciplines, urging clinicians to use their expertise to consult into different clinics and with different professional backgrounds within Tier 3 CAMHS. For those of you unfamiliar with the terminology, Tier 3 was (and remains) the service working with children and young people with significant mental health difficulties. So, the joint working in this instance was between Tier 3 and the Learning Disability/Complex Needs Service.

So that is where my exposure to these 'different' young women began. This is where I met Darcey, Milly and Esther. These extraordinary young women heavily influenced my clinical evolvement and opened my mind to a different kind of 'difference'.

It is important to acknowledge that the book is a reflective account of the young women's experiences of services and my experiences as a clinician working with them. These are personal accounts with statements that, I must stress, are not personal to individual clinicians or individual services, but are reflective of services nationally and worldwide which need to redefine their clinical pathways and ways of implementing clinical strategies and interventions for this group of individuals. There needs to be a service rethink, a fundamental understanding of need and an understanding of clinical presentation in order to reshape clinician's practices, beliefs, assessments and guidance. This will ensure a correct diagnosis with strategies to underpin the diagnosis for both the individual and their parents/carers and siblings. If this process is appropriate and accurate and delivered in the right way, it will, it is hoped, highlight the individual's qualities and strengths and have as part of the process some flexibility to use those identified skills and qualities to evolve those crucial elements needed in life's journey of building positive self-esteem, confidence and an understanding of self. This will, in turn then, enable young women to move forward after diagnosis, with pride and resilience and an ability to embrace, celebrate and manage their difference.

It's important for me also to mention that there were many young women in my career prior and following the three young women in this book. Those young women also experienced disjointed, sometimes inappropriate, services and interventions and, as my career has taken me to all parts of the country and the world experiencing the same problems with services, this evidences that the problems stretch far and wide.

All these girls and young women are the reason and foundation of this book, and the reason for highlighting the need to increase clinical understanding and expertise and identify the individual and service needs of girls and young women with ASC.

Many of these young women will have also experienced numerous referrals and interventions over numerous years and will have been asked to retell their stories repeatedly. Each episode of care would have tried therapies in vogue at the time, such as solution-focused brief therapy (SFBT), person-centred counselling and various types of questionnaires to ascertain mood and assessment of mood, all by the medium of talking. Others will have been referred for dialectical behaviour therapy (DBT), cognitive behaviour therapy (CBT) and been involved in behavioural interventions either placed upon them or around them and, on many occasions, these girls and young women would have 'disengaged' and would have been discharged without a service or an understanding or sometimes, more troubling, a *missed* or *misdiagnosis.*

These referrals would have included statements and judgements about parenting, anger issues, self-harm, eating difficulties, obsessional thinking, behaviours and aggressive outbursts and sometimes psychotic episodes, and would have led the young women and their families down diagnostic pathways that were unhelpful, and sometimes even inappropriate and misguided.

Eventually some of those girls and young women would have had their difficulties/needs recognised, sometimes through a period of elimination assessments, and would be offered an assessment for ASC, but some would never have got that far, left still wondering and/or struggling as to why they felt different; some will have taken their own lives or ended up on medications long term or may have been institutionalised; others may have entered the criminal justice system; others may to date be self-medicating with the use of alcohol or other substances and some may have engaged in risky behaviours which compromise their own and others' wellbeing. This is the reality for some of these young women and this is what I have experienced with some of the young women I have previously worked with and currently work with.

Some individuals' diagnoses come so late that they cannot access continued services and interventions due to service deficiencies/limitations, eligibility criteria and/or lack of trust in services. Some diagnostic pathways are not offered or available in certain areas of the country and some services do not have eligibility criteria for people who have received a diagnosis and need ongoing support, education and practical strategies in the form of advice and consultation. It is important to stress that eligibility criteria are also different. Specialist services are sparse, and even when you do get the specialist services, those deeper understandings of complex conditions are often not available as there are very few clinicians educated, trained and, more to the point, confident and motivated to work in this field.

Who would not be inspired to want to learn more and to want to practise in a specialism if you had the opportunity to watch and learn from such individuals?

Unfortunately, for some of these young women the years of being misunderstood, repeatedly, being asked to retell their stories, being repeatedly assessed and reassessed for mental health difficulties, with no true understanding of their complexities or their individuality, take a toll on their trust of services and clinicians. Family and schools experience difficulties in initially identifying the difference and then communicating in helpful ways with our young women, as they too struggle with building skills and knowledge and management strategies due to lack of support and resources; this then results in deterioration of emotional wellbeing for everyone involved. This unfortunately has a further impact of clinicians leaving this specialism and the services they work in.

This sounds harsh but *this is the reality*; this is still being seen repeatedly ten years on from my first experience of working with young women with ASC within a mental health setting *and this is about people's lives.*

To date referrals are received with these same patterns of difficulties, the same patterns of revolving in and out of services with unresolved issues, but as services we are slow to recognise and to respond accordingly to these patterns and trends: slow to identify need, slow to adapt assessments and interventions and slow to respond to the need. There is still a lazy approach to audit of referrals, especially around neurodevelopmental conditions within mental health. It is widely written about and researched that all behaviours and interactions have a function, and if there are misunderstandings or miscommunications on a repeated cycle this can significantly impact on individuals' emotional wellbeing and mental health. The consequences of *misdiagnosis, mismanagement* and *misunderstanding* impact and resonate on those individuals and their families for years.

What I continue to see is that often young women can disguise or mask their social abilities, but this ultimately does not protect them against the complexities of friendships and relationships in general, and it is often at this point when I come into contact with them, as the camouflaging has reached its capacity and the vulnerability is at its pinnacle.

I have been fortunate since my original experiences to have continued to meet and work with many young women, but the three I have already mentioned stood out. I recently met all three of the young women telling their stories in their homes with their families, having not seen them for many years. They all agreed to share their stories to ensure more helpful ways of working with the future generation of women with ASC, with more understanding of their differences.

I found myself captivated by their charisma and their ability to articulate their stories in a factual but very emotive way. I met them on their own personal journeys with their families, trying to be understood and to understand themselves. Their motivation to understand themselves and to be understood in the face of significant social and generalised anxiety, difficulties with social communication, interaction and social imagination, obsessional thinking and behaviour and inflexibility of thought was astonishing. Their passage of acceptance of themselves, their eventual understanding of their diagnosis and their eventual pride in themselves, of just that, being themselves, has been an honour to be part of and to watch unfold and evolve.

The current prevalence of autism is 1:100 (Baron-Cohen 2008) with approximately four affected males for every one affected female (Werling and Geschwind 2013):

> The current World Health Organization (WHO) international diagnostic criteria for autism do not give examples of the types of difficulties typically experienced by women and girls. (Pinto 2017)

So now is the time to change.

These three young women and their stories explain why I am passionate about working with girls and young women with autism.

Embedded through the book I will be walking you through the clinical aspects of the young women's experiences, some practical advice and some things to consider within your practice.

So, with all that said, I'd like to introduce you to Milly, Darcey and Esther.

CHAPTER 2

Milly, Darcey and Esther

MILLY

Milly's experiences are explained by her parents, with Milly's consent, as Milly has difficulty remembering these years.

Missed opportunities

Lisa: We had always considered Milly to be an obstinate (at times belligerent) child who struggled with socialising. I distinctly remember her infant teacher once telling me she was unable to coax Milly into doing something. I recall responding with words to the effect of 'welcome to my world', as this was a daily reality for us at home, but I believed she was generally compliant at school as, other than on this one occasion, I was not informed otherwise.

Obviously school must have had their concerns, which is why, a few years later, unbeknown to us, they enlisted the help of a specialist teacher. It was during one of these sessions that it was noticed Milly was unable to recognise emotions in a test of facial expressions printed on a sheet of paper. At this point it was suggested to us that she displayed some traits of ASC, but no follow-up was offered nor did I know what to do/where to go with that information (this being pre-home PCs or smartphones, and not something widely talked about in the media back then), so we left it hanging, assuming if there was an issue school would take care of making any necessary arrangements for further exploration. Nothing happened, it was never mentioned again and was forgotten about. This is not a criticism of the school, far from it, but with hindsight it could and should have been followed up. As Milly was our first-born, despite intuitively knowing things weren't 'right', we were not in a position to compare her to another child of our own. As a mother I had observed many other children at play over the years and was convinced Milly was 'different', but no one seemed to listen to our concerns, so we put her behaviour down to her 'individual' personality and got on with it as best we could. Her behaviour continued to be erratic and her over-reactions to things at times frightening, and eventually, out of desperation, we asked for help.

The referral process to CAMHS took months, during which time Milly was regularly 'running away' from home and talking about not wanting to be alive. We would pace the streets for hours, keeping a watchful eye from a safe distance to allow her to continue unhindered until finally she would choose to return home, sometimes with blisters on her feet. We had no idea what was going through her mind and no one to turn to.

Milly had been a difficult child from birth, persistently crying and nothing would appease her. Even the childminder remarked, at five months old, how determined a character she was. By the age of eight this stubborn determination had manifested itself into a worrying tendency of running away from home when things weren't going her way. Coupled with her stating she no longer wanted to live we sought professional help. It took till she was nine to initially be seen at CAMHS.

The health visitor advised the following, in a bid to stop her screaming/crying every morning when she woke up, the advice was to give Milly a positive phrase, 'I've had a lovely sleep', these words were repeated by Milly for months and months after the health visitor spoke to her. Whilst her behaviour improved slightly, the delivery and tone (bellowed at the top of her lungs) did not match the sentiment being expressed. She repeated the phrase verbatim every morning, without fail until we asked her to desist.

We surprised the kids one morning by saying, 'Let's go to the zoo today'. Big mistake to surprise Milly, I couldn't understand her reaction, most kids would be delighted at the prospect. Milly refused to come.

Milly's involvement with services spanned many years, *seven* to be precise. Milly's parents describe their and Milly's journey:

> *Lisa*: The initial CAMHS referral was in 2004, when Milly was nine years, one month old. The reason for the referral was that we struggled with Milly's behaviour at home. She would shut down for several days at a time, becoming uncommunicative and refusing to eat. She would storm off, and Andy would have to follow her through the streets for anything up to two hours at a time. She indicated that she hated her life and would prefer to be dead and talked about harming herself with a knife.
>
> The waiting time was up to six months for an appointment, and during this time I felt we were at risk of inflicting both physical and psychological damage on each other.

The referral highlighted the following parental concerns:

- low self esteem
- running away from home
- threatening to kill herself
- wanting to be dead
- frustration
- jealousy
- lack of confidence.

This was Andy (her dad's) description of the behaviours they were trying to understand and manage:

> She continues to display dogged persistence and determination and generally carries threats through.

> *Lisa*: At her initial appointment Milly was exceedingly stressed and anxious and proceeded to pick invisible floating flecks from the air whilst rocking in her seat. Milly's responses, if at all, were monosyllabic. We attended several sessions during which Milly's stress levels, if anything, worsened.

The sessions did not include practical strategies and the assessment was inconclusive. This left us feeling perplexed and frustrated that a specialist mental health service was unable to shed light on our ongoing concerns and somewhat relieved when they discharged us at not having to subject our child to more sessions but we felt let down by the service's lack of expertise, no further ahead in our understanding of our daughter, nor were we given any practical strategies to enable us to handle the sometimes unmanageable and distressed and distressing behaviour.

The second CAMHS referral was in 2006. Milly was ten years and five months old. The reason for the referral was:

Lisa: The situation at home had not improved, and desperation drove us once again to seek support. By then Milly was running away from perceived contaminants/dangerous substances (deodorant, cleaning products, etc.) and refusing to use glue at school; displaying obsessive compulsive disorder (OCD) tendencies, becoming very literal and obsessional in her thinking and her primary school had enlisted the help from a specialist teacher who advised us to seek a referral to CAMHS.

Age 11:

Lisa: Over six months after our referral was received we were eventually seen by a practitioner who appeared to listen and take an interest. Milly received the communication in a slightly less stressful manner but blatantly disliked the whole process and did not engage. Once again, no assessment was offered nor any attempt made to investigate Milly's situation. Various suggestions were offered as coping mechanisms for anxiety. These sessions once again came to an end and as they appeared largely valueless we made no attempt to fight for their continuation.

Milly's third referral to CAMHS was in February 2009, when Milly was 13 years and seven months old. The referral came from Milly's general practitioner (GP, family doctor) regarding deterioration at school in terms of reaching her potential and increased social isolation. Milly's parents reported that Milly:

- had extreme difficulty in coping with the unknown, where the loss and or lack of control either results in her becoming very withdrawn for days, even weeks on end, or unrestrained verbal, sometimes physical, outbursts

- displayed a lack of empathy and had formed no apparent friendships

- often appeared solemn, serious and unhappy, with low self-esteem

- was impossible to interpret, so they were therefore unable to help her tackle what they perceived as unreasonable behaviour.

There was additional information that at primary school teachers had queried Asperger syndrome (AS) and OCD, and there was some information about a paternal aunt with mental health difficulties.

The next appointment after this was when Milly was 13 years and 11 months old. This was the appointment that was to address the concerns around ASC.

> *Lisa*: In this first appointment of this referral with a mental health practitioner we were asked to complete and submit the following:
>
> - complex social communication team consultation form
>
> - questionnaires (multiple)
>
> - handwritten scenarios
>
> - supportive evidence for educational psychology
>
> - summary of information to support ASC pathway assessment.
>
> Once again, in a downward spiral of behaviours at home, I had sought help again. This time I arranged it on my own as my husband refused to attend, as he felt there was neither value nor support to be had from bureaucratic and incompetent services accessed via considerable difficulty. By the time the

appointment arrived I had had an epiphany and 'worked out' with the assistance of Google that Milly almost certainly had ASC. I arrived armed with the 'knowledge' and understandably was hesitant about sharing this with the professionals, expecting to be, if not ridiculed, then at the very least frowned upon for effectively self-diagnosing and telling the experts their job. I found it both liberating (our bad parenting may finally be exonerated) but equally distressing. I had always assumed Milly was just a hard nut to crack and somewhere buried deep inside would be her emotional core that no one had yet been privy to, but one day it would emerge and we'd make peace. Instead, knowing nothing about ASC, the future looked bleak. We couldn't cure her.

Andy described their concerns as parents:

As ever our main concern is for Milly's wellbeing and, reluctant as we are to have her labelled, we recognise that she struggles socially and the older she becomes the wider the gap between her and her peers appears. Her behaviour at times is intolerable and she has been known to resort to physical violence. We would like to attribute this to teenage angst but we are unsure whether her unreasonable behaviour has a different root cause. Most concerning is the detrimental effect this is having on our entire family.

Lisa reflects on the benefits of an ASC assessment:

Lisa: On the contrary, Fiona and another clinician listened, while I went through everything again, for the third time, full history and so on. Fiona explained the process that an ASC assessment would entail and asked me if I was sure I wanted to go down this route. I recall my response being along the lines of we had nothing to lose, we desperately needed help, I was at my wits end and needed to have our concerns finally taken seriously. I distinctly remember meeting Andy for lunch following the appointment in a bid to get him 'on board'. I managed to convince him that we could be getting somewhere this time as I felt Fiona, despite not having yet met with Milly, actually wanted to help us rather than just fulfil her duty. And you know how the story ends...

Milly was finally diagnosed with ASC in November 2009, when she was 14 years and four months old.

Lisa: Seven years from initial referral to diagnosis. This is not a criticism but a true explanation of what happened. This is real life and this is about my family.

At this point it may be helpful to reflect from a clinical perspective what might have been helpful to have expedited further understanding of Milly at that time, so we can start to see where clinical practice and service provision can be enhanced.

- Investigating the function/reason for the behaviour would have added relevant and vital information to have been explored at the stage of initial referral.

- Appropriately trained clinicians with a working knowledge of ASC in girls and young women are needed, as part of the initial assessment process.

- Observations need to be undertaken at home and school as reporting of behaviours can differ dramatically due to differing circumstances or environments, mainly due to socially masking and mimicking and a necessity not to be seen as different.

- Information gathering from all settings, not just home and school, is paramount, as it gives a holistic picture, as do different individuals within those settings: in different settings different behaviours and characteristics may be present.

- Behaviours cannot be assumed to be something unless evidenced to be so.

- If there are repeated referrals, look at the reasons and differences and what worked and what didn't the last time; this will inform practice by collating information.

- Repeatedly asking for information already shared can be distressing and exhausting and can impact on those initial stages of your therapeutic relationship and engagement, so collate as much as you can prior to reviewing.

- Match referral need with an appropriate skill mix of clinicians and if this is difficult discuss referral within a multi-disciplinary arena.

- We need to avoid young people suffering for extensive periods of time in their childhood by increasing our understanding and skill base to ensure speedy access to appropriate services.

Seven years is a massive chunk out of a child's life. Milly has since shared with me that she was distressed for most of this time. This must be remedied so other young women don't experience the difficulties Milly and her family faced in order to get an understanding and a diagnosis.

An important thing to note would be that, from a clinical perspective, you will never be able to enable an individual to manage and understand their emotions and behaviour if they don't understand themselves. And, as a clinician, how can you enable, support and advise if you don't know what you are trying to help them manage?

DARCEY

Here is Darcey's parents' first account of their daughter's difficulties and subsequent involvement with services.

> *Kelly and Ashley*: We first noticed unusual behaviour at the age of two to three years old. This was our first child, and we accepted these as behavioural difficulties that every parent expects. However, at the age of four Darcey was clearly showing signs of OCD. On one occasion, Darcey refused to sit down on a plane due to take off. By some miracle I identified a speck of cotton on the seat, and by covering it with my cardigan resolved the problem immediately, to the relief of surrounding passengers and cabin crew from Darcey's screaming. All attempts to discipline Darcey in her growing up, such as the 'naughty step'

and doing without treats for bad behaviour had very severe consequences in her reaction, namely complete meltdowns that she was able to sustain for long periods. We had no option but to relent on these occasions and pick our battles carefully. This was difficult when her younger sister could observe Darcey's dysfunctional behaviour and see a lack of follow through on her discipline, feeling life was just not fair when her sister was allowed to get away with things that she never would. In fact, it was the contrast between Darcey's behaviour and that of our other daughter Freya that began to raise suspicions that Darcey had behavioural difficulties.

By the age of eight, we were desperate for help and turned to the GP who referred us to CAMHS (November 2007). However, they did not accept the referral and suggested local parenting/behaviour management courses! This was obviously disappointing as it inferred that it was our 'parenting' that was at fault. We continued to handle Darcey's behaviour and meltdowns ourselves but this was taking its toll particularly on me and so once again we looked to the GP for help. This time our GP referred us to a consultant paediatrician and we secured an appointment in September 2009.

What could we learn from this account?

- One of the early signs we now know, particularly in girls, is repetitive obsessional thinking and behaving differently.

- Examine the parenting, the styles, the capacity of the parents, but don't just fall in to a trap of thinking the problem is parenting; dig deeper, observe their parenting, listen to how they report information to you, look at how they manage their own lives. If the child has siblings note how they parent them and how the sibling is developing.

- Examine the reaction and intensity to the 'norm' parenting and the impact on parenting styles.

- Look at the strategies parents and carers must put in place in order to remedy a situation/meltdown. Measure that against the norm and how other siblings would respond and be managed.

- Listen to parents when they give you clues in the information sharing, particularly when they explain about differences in siblings and how they have adapted to manage.

- Six years of support, understanding and advice was lost. Fortunately, this family were resilient and had good supportive networks and worked together well to support their daughter. They have therefore been able to continue to consistently parent and have the successful emotionally well daughter they have today. But there are families with their own difficulties, no support and limited resilience on whom trying to understand their child for six years would have taken its toll and the outcome will be, and has been evidenced from my own clinical experience, catastrophically different.

- Six years of the child developing behaviour patterns and their own ways of coping will be entrenched, thus making it harder for them to adapt and change, and for the parents and the clinician to find ways of motivating change and shifting belief systems.

- The importance of early intervention for the individual and the family is vital.

ESTHER

Here is Esther's parents' account of the lead up to diagnosis:

Ruth: We were lucky. I don't think Esther would have been diagnosed if her Year 2 (ages 6–7) teacher who had worked with autistic children hadn't transferred to her school to be her teacher. The school she was in for primary, and the one she subsequently went to for junior, did not appear to have the knowledge to have been able to spot autism. That teacher was only there for one year. We didn't notice the issues with Esther until she went to school. She was very shy and didn't like to be hugged and kissed, but that was her choice. At birthday parties, she didn't play with others and wanted to stay with me, but I put that down to shyness. At nursery, no issues were raised.

She didn't like circle time but nothing that stood out as different. In reception class (ages 4–5) at school I was told that Esther liked to watch activities before she would join in. A quote on her report said that, 'She is very amenable and compliant but on occasions has shown us that she can be very different!' I wish now I'd gone back and dug a little deeper on that comment.

In Year 1 (ages 5–6) I was told by a teaching assistant that 'Esther was the stubbornist child she had ever dealt with'.

I do remember a certain number of visits to the head teacher for refusing to do work that year and work destroyed. Lots of sticker plans with rewards to encourage her to work were put in place. None of which helped. She was an avid reader, though. Easily finishing all their reading plans.

When Esther's Year 2 class teacher tried to talk to her at the start of the year, one of Esther's class mates told her that Esther didn't speak. The teacher noted that Esther would turn her back, refuse to speak, destroy her work, and there was a lack of interaction with her class mates. Esther also reacted badly to changes in routine. Esther's teacher talked to her previous class teachers who said they had noticed things but hadn't felt confident enough to raise an issue.

Esther's teacher asked me to come in and sat me down and told me she thought Esther had autism. I think she expected a negative reaction from me, but for reasons I won't go into it was a relief. This was around the beginning of the school year, so in September or October 2009.

The school contacted the educational psychologist, and she worked with Esther from February to June 2010 initially. I'm afraid the experience with her was a negative one for me. I felt that all I was told was what Esther wouldn't do. This included writing with a pen, so I was to encourage her keyboard skills. Most of the advice was about making Esther comply with what was required rather than supporting her. The psychologist did arrange extra transition support for Esther to move from primary to junior school (ages 7–11). I seem to remember a booklet with pictures, so Esther could remember what the school was like over the holidays. The big negative was that, at the end of the year, when I asked her if she thought Esther had autism, she turned around and said it wasn't her job to diagnose and that she'd told me at the beginning I would have to go to my doctor for that. I'm pretty sure she didn't tell me to go to the doctor, as I would have acted on that advice. I was angry we'd lost a whole year and it meant we seemed to miss out on funding, as rules seemed to change the whole way through junior school.

I seem to remember the doctor being fine about the referral, as she was seeing the educational psychologist and school was recognising a problem, he referred her straight to CAMHS.

What can we learn from this account?

- Acknowledge, respect and work with other professionals who have expertise in this area too.

- Notice and explore comments about being 'shy' and 'different' within the context of other behaviours noted.

- Notice the words and comments being used to describe the girl/young woman: 'stubborn', 'watching', 'refusing to speak', 'damaging work'.

- Look at the function and context and shift in behaviours from compliant to not speaking and damaging own work.

- Look at areas they excel in.

- Be aware if usual age appropriate/mainstream reward systems don't work.

- Be confident to raise concerns and ask for help when you recognise clinical features when others in other professions don't.

- There is a need for professionals outside the diagnostic teams to be aware of and trained in different presentations and they can refer, consult or request support.

- Don't just think of something to solve the problem, investigate what the problem is. For example, 'difficulty using a pen so offered a keyboard'. What was the difficulty? In what settings? Explore physical difficulties, learning difficulties and, even if this may be the outcome in the end, at least you will have checked and identified why the problem was there in the first place which could lead to further questioning, observations and assessments. But the solution must come after questions, observations and assessments, not as a reaction to fixing an unknown origin of a problem.

- Increased multi-agency working and training only enriches understanding, it can never hinder an understanding.

For me there are many fundamental steps we still miss as clinicians and professionals working in this complex field of work. We look to fix rather than investigate. We put sticking plasters on but don't check the origin of the difficulty. This is due to many factors: how we are trained, service limitations, time restraints and waiting lists. It feels uncomfortable to acknowledge it but it is true and reflective of current service provision.

As individuals, these girls and young women have tremendous potential to be assets to the workforce and to society in general. Their intelligence, determination and tenacity is often what is lacking in business, relationships and industries.

However, these strengths and qualities are often hindered by underlying significant generalised and social anxiety, obsessional and ritualistic tendencies, which sometimes overwhelm them and interrupt and sometimes cease their learning, performance and relationships. Sensory difficulties can impact on being able to access environments or be taught by particular members of staff. Impulsivity, difficulties with emotional dysregulation and executive functioning, alongside a strong sense of their own interpretation of the moral code can interrupt learning and social situations.

The impact on their difficulties if they are misunderstood can be so detrimental to their whole wellbeing and social input. If they are understood, supported and enabled at an early age, their life stories can be so different, so positive, so fruitful, so rewarding.

When young women revolve in and out of mental health services numerous times continuing to express and display emotional distress, anger, obsessional and sometimes significant self-harm and concerning deterioration in their mood and behaviour, questions need to be asked as to where the fundamental root or function of the distress lies. We as the assessors need to look deeper as there is always a reason. Remember, girls can mask, they can present as more socially alert and aware and their symptomology is subtler not only in its presentation but in its function/origin.

Here are a few examples from my own experience of things often not recognised or implemented:

- Look for the difference in thinking, as there are many types with many qualities.

- Use the individual's ability to see detail, as in certain arenas this is of huge benefit.

- This may seem trivial but it is actually fundamental in a social world: the importance of learning manners and being respectful.

- Be aware of specialist minds. Being good at some things and not so good at others doesn't mean the good bits can't be developed and nurtured.

- Sensory issues: for some individuals on the spectrum their sensory difficulties impact hugely on their everyday functioning as well as their emotional management and resilience. These can sometimes be mistaken for lack of focus and concentration and hyperactivity and anxiety. Their experiences can help us modify all types of environments.

- It is important that teachers and clinicians learn about the special interests and motivators of young people they work with. Work with their different ways of thinking, including making education more flexible. Mentors are essential and integral in being 'that go to person' when things become difficult or unmanageable. This element can be the make or break of a young person still accessing their services.

- Early intervention is crucial if you are to enable basic behaviours to assist individuals trying to cope in a world that thinks differently to them. It is also essential to enable appropriate self-emotional regulation.

- Stretch the fixation, use interests/motivators as tools to encourage the individual to manage situations and conversations. If you use these you can practise skills such as reciprocity, which will be helpful when reciprocity is needed in order to assist an interaction or a relationship.

- Learn social skills through play/role play, give immediate reflection on an interaction, whether positive or negative, and practise in the real world. Doing the basics in appointments is fine, but if you are to enable your young person in wider contexts they need to practise out and about so they can generalise. This means you need those around them to implement these strategies, which in turn means more training.

- Encourage interactions with others with shared interests.

- Watch out for Alexithymia.

Temple Grandin is a perfect example of a woman with autism who is continually trying to understand and manage her difficulties, not only for her own benefit but to increase awareness and understanding of this complex condition: an extraordinary woman who has had a huge impact on my choice of clinical path. Her never-ending growth of her understanding of the condition and herself and her ability to communicate her findings with the rest of the world have enthused and entranced everyone who has met her or listened to her or read her books or articles.

CHAPTER 3

Beginning with Relationships

'It was nice to be treated like the individual I am, and not like I was trying to be placed in some meaningless tick boxes.'

(Milly)

The relationship must start with respect and interest. The clinician should treat the young woman as a person in her own right. Move into their world; once you do you will start to see the relationship shift, and they will start to trust you. Eventually they will start to sometimes join you in your world for a while. It may be brief and fleeting initially, but it will happen and you will feel the shift and difference in your relationship. Then you know you have commenced a relationship with them.

It is now up to you as their clinician to guide and support them. They are almost always motivated to understand themselves – why they think and act like they do – and then learn how to manage their differences in a positive and helpful way to enable them to be the best of themselves. However, sometimes this is not evident at the onset as they are confused, scared, anxious and angry. Labels are often a no go area, especially labels which conjure up images of something which seems so far removed from them that it is unrecognisable and frightening. The need for sameness also becomes a barrier, as with a label can come prejudice, discrimination, disbelief and misunderstanding.

It is to be hoped that what these young women will enter into and experience is the journey of acceptance of diagnosis, and the positivity it can provide, if understood, within an individual context, and communicated in the same vein to those who are important in their lives.

MILLY

Milly is a complex and intelligent young woman. It took months to get to a point where Milly accepted me being in her life; after all, she had experienced numerous clinician relationships along the way which to her and her family were not the most positive or helpful. We had many times where there were no words, hostility and upset, but we also had times where we laughed and even got to the point of me being able to joke with Milly about something very personal to her and poignant in terms of social communication and interaction. Let me explain: Milly could express very clearly with her facial expression when she was not happy with something I said or was asking her to do. We got to the point where I could say, 'You've got the Milly face on!' We only got to this point as we had built enough mutual trust and respect for me to be able to be straight and blunt about something Milly had great difficulty doing, showing appropriately how she was feeling and what she was thinking. Through this we worked on how her facial expressions and body language impacted on others, and what that means in terms of building relationships, and being understood. I was mindful to be sensitive to Milly's thoughts and feelings in times when conversations were emotional and heated, as well as supporting her family with their worries and upset.

Challenging parents and the young person is occasionally needed in order for them to grow in their understanding and acceptance of what is happening to and around them. At this point in their clinical journey, however inclusive you make it, things happen to the client, and some of this is out of everyone's control but is needed to move processes forward. Challenging needs to be implemented, however, with great care and empathy; you are present in people's lives at their most vulnerable and raw. If you succeed, however, you see them develop and manage in a more helpful way for themselves as individuals and their family members. Finding the balance is imperative, as these families must continue to function and thrive after you leave their lives. The chances are that these particular families will come across services related to the diagnosis time and time again at points in their lives, so their experience needs to be positive and beneficial.

These young women's families in most cases are crucial in continuing and sustaining emotional wellbeing for ther daughters; they need support, nurturing and understanding as much as their children/siblings.

> *Lisa*: I didn't feel as if you judged me, I felt as if you empathised with the tough time we were going through and wanted to help us all as a family. We knew we weren't perfect as parents, and you weren't afraid to tell us when we'd got it wrong (usually me) which I respected you for. I might not have liked hearing it at the time, but I knew that you would only say such things to help us. You made us feel our concerns were valid and worked collaboratively with us to improve things. You seemed to understand how hard it was and to genuinely care. Having the support of someone who, in Milly's words, 'got it' made it easier to bear. You knew I didn't want the outcome we got, but having the diagnosis meant that the strategies you gave us could help and, ultimately, I felt vindicated and no longer (totally) 'to blame' for Milly's behaviour.

Add-on from Andy:

> Your predecessors were lacking in knowledge, interest and passion to guide and support us and were perhaps out of their depth. I came away from both of our previous experiences of the service feeling I knew more than they did and that it was just a case of going through the motions but with little intent to obtain the right outcome.

The therapeutic relationship is crucial in the whole process as this enables trust, confidence and understanding, and mutual respect, which in turn dominoes into collaboratively enabling the young women's self-exploration, reflection, observation of self and others and growth into self-management and maintenance of emotional wellbeing.

To ensure success of the therapeutic relationship the following elements from my experience are vital, and I see it as like a jigsaw.

TIME

This refers not only to clinic time/appointment time but to length of the intervention. As clinicians, we are pushed for contacts and throughput, but we are not dealing with inanimate objects, we are working with human beings who are experiencing distress and who need time. Of course, we must be mindful of the duration and frequency of appointments and open episodes of care, but this not only relies on the expertise of us as clinicians, it relies on effective systems. The systems need to underpin and support the therapeutic interventions in order that all parties benefit. Efficient and quality interventions such as timely assessments and reviews result in more young people being seen in a more productive and helpful way.

COMPASSION

This should come naturally to us all, but that is often not true and can sometimes be because of the impact of clinician's stress. These stressors come from frustration at lack of others in the system understanding the complexity of work, and time that needs to be invested in ensuring a productive excellent service is offered to our young people. We also have to remember that we are human and our own personal lives are running parallel to our work lives. Some of us have more compassion than others and that is natural; either way, don't forget about it and try to practise it as, after all, these young people are in a specialist service as they are experiencing significant levels of distress, and we are there to offer them a humanitarian service.

RESPECT

We need to take each young person we see as an individual and see them first as a person and their difficulties as secondary. Due to the complexity of the clinical presentation we sometimes see our young people display behaviours which make us feel disrespected, but we need to understand this in the context of their difficulties and complexity. *Don't excuse it but understand it.* Too often clinicians expect respect, but we have to earn it; we are offering a service.

EXPERTISE

In a time of financial restraint and continuing professional development being sparse, we are becoming a service that is stunted and not growing in expertise. In order to deliver excellence, we need to learn and grow and develop in our specialities. This can be done in many ways, but so many of those ways are hindered by other issues such as numbers and throughput; rarely do we have the luxury to shadow each other and work into different disciplines or offer consultation appointments. These elements need to be encouraged as they are quick wins. Clinicians who are excellent in their fields should impart their knowledge and expertise to others. As mentioned earlier, this is how I met these young women. A skilled and experienced manager saw the benefits of joining expertise. It may seem extravagant but with complexity comes a need for flexible and diverse ways of working.

ENVIRONMENT

Clinic rooms and noisy interview rooms in schools are often the hardest places for our young people to concentrate, relax and engage with the therapeutic alliance or therapy. We know that we are often dealing with young women with extreme anxiety, yet we ask them to attend a place which may smell weird or be susceptible to echoing; to sit in a crowded waiting room with other young people they may know, whom they would prefer they don't know they are attending a specialist service. Home visits are frowned upon in terms of lone working and risk and time, but it is down to good assessments and communication on behalf of the clinician to ensure their own safety is assured before venturing on a home visit. They are also time consuming, often taking longer. However, the counterargument is that if you use them for those who really need it, then at least you get engagement rather than non-attendance and therefore a delayed positive outcome. We should be implementing more mindful environments and using our young people's motivators. Milly, for example, was so anxious about her autism diagnostic schedule (ADOS) that we went to her home on two separate occasions, once to plan the most suitable part of the house to do an assessment in, and second to ensure it was the best place for Milly to have her assessment. This enabled us to get the best out of Milly to inform our assessment appropriately. Go for walks, sit in the playground, do some gardening, find the most helpful environment: then the rest will start to fall into place.

EMPATHY

It's always difficult to put yourself in someone's else's shoes, but we have all been scared or anxious or sad or frightened. We have all experienced these feelings in our lives, so we need to draw on those experiences and feelings and how we responded at the time in order to enable us to have empathy on those occasions when our young people can't, for example, access the building, the room or the therapy. Be kind, be patient, adapt your approach.

UNDERSTANDING

Communicate to your young person that you can wait, that you can empathise, observe and respond to ensure you support them in the most helpful way at that time. Reassure them, don't judge, don't be dismissive, don't criticise. Reassure their parents/carers. Keep calm and be flexible and responsive to their needs at the time.

INDIVIDUALISED CARE

This is very important. We are all individuals. We do not fit into boxes.

BE HUMANE

Incorporate all of the above by being compassionate, kind, understanding, tolerant, empathic, sympathetic, fair and considerate.

This is one of Milly and her parents' initial experiences of an appointment:

> *Lisa*: When she was finally given an appointment, the meeting was excruciating to watch. She sat rocking in a chair and picking invisible 'flecks' out of the air. It felt as if she was being interrogated, and she couldn't answer the questions that were being put to her. She was asked to gauge her feelings on a scale. She was only aged nine or ten. After just a few more sessions, where no progress was made we were told we'd had our allotted quota and sent packing.

Milly beautifully describes a positive, helpful, enabling, therapeutic relationship:

> It was so important to feel a connection with someone who was there to help, and I didn't feel like a number in a system, I felt like a person who mattered, and who was actually cared about.

Lisa explains:

> Up until this point no one had ever been able to read Milly. She had no facial expressions and did not care to be around other children, preferring instead the company of adults.

The fundamentals of being humane can be achieved within our clinical and service constraints; they *can* work symbiotically.

The basics of an effective reciprocal therapeutic alliance which hopefully becomes mutually beneficial is the same whatever background you come from clinically or otherwise. At the end of the day we are describing a relationship. Some individuals (clinicians) are naturals at building relationships, but some are not, and those who struggle with this element should ensure they are either skilled enough to manage it or use their skills in different ways.

Our ages and where and when we were trained also impact on the way we embrace the relationship. It's a fine line between being too familiar and being professional but friendly and open. This can be hard, and it will at times move and shift, as all relationships do. The important thing is to address these shifts and changes and move helpfully through them.

At these times it is imperative you seek guidance and clinical supervision. This may seem an obvious point to make, but due to the drivers currently in place it is all too easy for a clinician to interpret a problem with the relationship as a reason to cease treatment. And, yes, sometimes this is the case; often we need to work harder, more sensitively and adapt and shift our way of working or change the clinician. This would obviously be a last resort but at least it should be considered and explored.

> *Lisa*: We continued to muddle through as best we could, but the crises were coming thick and fast. My other daughter (younger) and I frequently avoided coming home after school, hanging around the library for as long as possible, because we were afraid of what we might encounter from Milly at home. Once again, we went through the long referral process, filling out copious forms yet again and giving a full history and were finally seen again by someone different. Whilst this clinician appeared to listen to our concerns more earnestly, the process hadn't changed, with Milly being asked to mark where she was feeling on a scale each week. We went through the motions but had lost faith we were ever going to be taken seriously. All the while behaviours at home were escalating. Once again, we were discharged with no real progress having been made and we felt utterly defeated by the system.
>
> By the time we had our third referral to CAMHS my husband had given up hope, and I went alone, initially without Milly. Once again, I ran through the full history and my concerns, but on this occasion, I suggested AS as a possible reason for her behaviours. As a parent and lay person, it is difficult to tell a professional what you think may lie at the route of the problem, but I felt I had nothing left to lose. Milly was not in a good way, and as a family we were all struggling. The implications of the assessment route were explained to me and, as Milly was

now 14, I had to get her consent. It was a difficult decision to choose the route of potential diagnoses, particularly as Milly was now going through puberty, which in itself presented problems. Finally, we were being listened to and this led on to a diagnosis but, more importantly, the support we received offered us strategies as to how best to live to get through this and support our daughter. We were educated as to what AS means and accordingly were able to (not always successfully) vary our approach to reduce Milly's anxieties. This in turn made for a more harmonious existence for all of us.

Izzy, Milly's sister, writes so eloquently of how this whole episode in her life affected and impacted on her as a younger sister:

Much of our time together as a family used to be fraught and tense, especially in the years before Milly's diagnosis. While she could be loving and kind, her apparently random changes in temperament frightened me, she could go from being perfectly pleasant to cruel and bitter within the space of a few minutes. Sometimes it got really bad at home. My mum often used to pick me up from school and take me straight to the library or supermarket, so we could delay going home for as long as possible. I struggled with conflict and therefore used to consistently do my sister's bidding, despite calls from my parents to stand up to her. I knew from a very young age that refusing to obey her would lead to a physical battle or a cold silence which would hang over the house like a storm cloud.

Nonetheless, I adored my big sister and greatly admired her intelligence and wit. I knew she would protect me and defend me if necessary, and it was obvious that she loved her family no matter what she often said. I do have many fond childhood memories with her, although we have definitely got on better since she was diagnosed and given proper help.

The relationship is not only with the clinician doing the direct work but everything that spirals off from that. The relationship is with the family members and then with the service. The relationship starts with the letter, the receptionist, the environment, not just the clinician. It's a huge responsibility, as our actions impact on so many people's lives. We should always remember that how we should treat people is how we and our loved ones would expect to be treated ourselves, and therefore understand that when people can't access the things we offer them they are sometimes angry and frustrated. Work through these times with your individuals and families, whilst always ensuring you are safe within that, this means emotionally and physically.

> *Lisa*: You listened to our concerns and, as Andy just said to me, 'actually knew something'! Whereas our previous experience had been a one-size-fits-all, limited number of sessions, an exercise in ticking a box: you get referred, you get seen, you get discharged and that's it, we've fulfilled our obligation regardless of whether we've made any difference.

My relationship with Milly and her family from my perspective was built on respect, patience, honesty, experience and, yep, knowing my stuff and being confident and empathic when delivering it. Milly and her family were in a place of confusion, frustration and fear of the unknown, so we were starting from a difficult place therapeutically, as trust had been challenged, as had clinical expertise. Being kind and sensitive was the order of the day and being confident in my knowledge and skills. Milly and her parents not only needed reassurance that I knew what I was doing, but that I was going to do what I said I would do. They needed me to be well informed and compassionate to their circumstances.

These were intelligent, articulate, kind people who had parented well and who deserved the best I could give as a clinician and as a person. I therefore at times shared some of my own life experiences with them, mindful of the professional boundaries, I might add. Again, I used my experience to gauge how much to share and what was appropriate in the context of the support and advice I was giving them on their situation. I'm always very mindful that I am entering into their lives and this should come with some humanity. These individuals and family members are sharing the most sensitive and personal information with me and allowing me to see them at their most raw. They know I hold information on them and that is a very vulnerable place to be. I always try to imagine how I would cope in a similar situation and how I would expect to be treated. I took considerable time to include all the most relevant and important people in Milly's life and asked for their views and opinions. I visited them in their home when it was needed. I spent time with family members, listening and supporting their needs at that difficult time. I empathised with Milly's sister and listened to her accounts of the impact on her and her relationship with her sister. I ensured that there were times when I could meet with Andy, which meant working late in late clinics, but this enabled Milly's dad to be involved and to have his voice heard. If this had not been an option, Andy would not have been involved, and I would have missed vital information and a chance to information share and support a vital member of the family.

In Milly's case, there was more work with all members of the family, sometimes as a family, but also with them individually, than with Milly on her own. Milly found it more difficult and less helpful doing one-to-one sessions using talking therapies. She was better with her mum and or dad reflecting on an incident/situation and working it through, listening to others' viewpoints and opinions. Milly trusted me (after a time) to talk to her teachers about her and to ask them about her, but preferred not to be present when I did that. She was always attentive and respectful when I fed back these meetings to her, although mostly in disagreement with what I fed back on their behalf.

Eventually I began to feel a warmth from Milly towards me. This would mostly be via her fantastic humour or by a tiny little smile or some meaningful interchanges. Milly was challenging for me as a clinician, as she gave me nothing for months. However, when she did engage, it was wonderful, and I was privy to a Milly I knew she would allow herself to be one day. A beautiful, intelligent, interesting and warm young woman. Now, after meeting with her recently, I can certainly confirm she is all of the above, with some additional qualities of resilience, tenacity, determination and courage.

Initially I listened and was compassionate and patient.

Then I informed, challenged and supported.

And then educated, empathised and enabled.

DARCEY

Darcey's presentation was one of frustration and anger underpinned with immense determination and motivation to understand herself and be understood. She was not angry at or with me. She was angry at why people didn't understand her and why they didn't adapt to her. She was rigid in her thoughts and beliefs but also highly anxious. She was ultimately confused by the world around her; as she was so intelligent the world and people should have made sense to her, but it and they didn't.

Darcey was delightful to work with on a clinical and individual level. She was open to any suggestions of how she could understand herself and others better and how she could enable others to understand her in a meaningful way. She was motivated to learn about herself and her diagnosis and embraced it fully. She was intelligent and driven.

When it came to family work to support Darcey and to aid understanding of Darcey this was more difficult for her. She worked better on a one-to-one or two-to-one basis. Also her sister Freya was younger, and having long sessions talking and reflecting about her sister's antics in the previous week was tough for her. It has to be said, though, that Freya was mature for her age and patient and often spent a long time waiting in the waiting area or the car for the session to finish. Darcey had and still has very different relationships with her parents, both extremely supportive and loving but different. Now the difference is very much more understood and embraced by all of the family members, but at the time Darcey tended to be better working things out with each of them separately.

Understanding all these dynamics is essential to ensuring the sessions you do are the most helpful to that individual, not what we think is best, or because that is the current trend of working or the only option. Our clinical relationship was strengthened by the fact that the sessions were adapted to fit the needs of Darcey – Darcey was aware of this and responded well to the way her sessions were organised.

She engaged well from the start with me and the process and we built a strong, mutually respectful and warm relationship, mainly through drawing, the use of externalisation and sessions with Darcey's parents where we would reflect on concerns or worries, in order to understand those worries and concerns and implement ways of managing situations in a more productive and helpful way for all concerned. Darcey tolerated coming to the CAMHS building well and always participated fully and positively in her time with me.

Darcey wanted to communicate. Initially what she needed in order to benefit from any future clinical interventions was to be understood in order to enable her to manage her emotions in a more appropriate and helpful way.

> *Darcey*: I had a good relationship with Fiona, and I liked the one-to-one rather than all together as it allowed me to open up more. Having the relationship made me trust Fiona which meant I would say a lot more stuff about how I feel and stuff that's happened and not feel scared or embarrassed. Fiona really understood me and wouldn't judge. It's hard for someone like me to explain how I feel or just explain things, so it's most important to have a good relationship with your one-to-one and for them to understand about Asperger's, to be able to help me describe how I feel or let me open up. The activities we did together were also beneficial and a good way to help me understand myself and everything alongside. It was never intimidated at any point I think?? Other than with other people such as the psychiatrist man who did games and tests in the one-way mirror.

She had already started ballet and was excelling at this; this gave me evidence that she had many strengths and was able to express her emotions and communicate through dance. She also had started to make her own animations. As her clinician I needed to use these strengths and examples to demonstrate and emphasise to her what she could do and not to concentrate and focus on what she couldn't do.

Initially I observed and listened and gathered information.

Then I used clinical expertise and Darcey's intelligence and motivation to enable understanding and management of specific emotions.

And then I educated, empathised and enabled the individual, the family and the teachers.

ESTHER

Esther was a young girl experiencing a world of misunderstanding and misinterpretation when I met her. What was striking about her from the onset was the ways she had found to manage her distress. Esther did not speak at times, words did not flow with her, especially at times of distress. She would use objects of interest to her to enable to manage difficult situations and transition her from one place/situation to another. Books were very important, as were other favourite toys and objects. But Esther had a wonderfully cheeky side to her and a fabulous sense of humour.

Esther's and my relationship was about trust. I knew I would need to reach further towards Esther as she was having significant difficulties with her ability to express herself in a way others would understand. Esther also needed time to process and for everything to be calm and slowed down. Her obsessions/motivators were significant in her life, so I would need to understand, accept and use them if I were to have a chance of any sort of relationship with Esther. Observing these needs of Esther's was imperative in our relationship. I knew I would have to be especially patient and mindful of how I conducted myself and my sessions with Esther. I was acutely aware that, if I were to gain her trust, my knowledge of her would need to be translated into school as this was the place at that time which was causing her so much anguish.

With Esther I had to make a lot of scaffolding to our relationship, and it took time. These are the times when trying to evidence the importance of the therapeutic alliance to the demands of the systems and expectations of commissioners and so on is hard. But time spent now at such a crucial point in a young person's emotional and educational development will benefit them and future care and provision. If you get it right and enable emotional resilience early on then the impact on services at a later date is going to be much less, if needed at all. I built on the work done previously by a colleague, which had been an excellent foundation and platform for Esther to start to explore anger and how to understand and manage it in a more helpful way to her and then for others.

With Esther it was important that she had her mum with her in her sessions. Esther's mum, Ruth, was often in the early days of our work together the communication conduit. She would guide me as to how far I could take Esther in the session, and would offer strategies and advice to me and reassurance and support to Esther to assist in ensuring we had a helpful and productive session. This was vital and hugely important to all of us. Esther's family were/are extremely important to her. They understand her difficulties exceptionally well and enable and support her to manage them whilst continually communicating their pride in her as a young woman and as their daughter. They were integral in Esther accessing her sessions at CAMHS and in enabling me to communicate with school.

> *Ruth, dictated from Esther*: I think the fact that you and I got on well was vital. Esther says that being valued by you was important and the fact that you didn't judge her but just tried to help when school was just not understanding at all. School didn't go out of their way to help, they were just bothered about what went on the report. She didn't feel any pressure to be better. She could just be herself with you. No pressure to use things suggested in sessions, just tools to use if she wanted to. If something wasn't useful you tried to find something else to use to help.

SUMMARY

As you can see from my descriptions, all three young women had the same difficulties and challenges but they impacted and manifested and presented differently.

This is where the relationship is vital. You can know about autism but that alone will not help you when you are faced with the individual needs of that child/young person sitting in front of you in significant distress. It's more important to understand the impact on the individual and their families and how this can be addressed and understood and how to tackle that with each individual in the best way for them. And the relationship is not just with your young person. It extends to anyone or anything who is significant in their life, including significant others outside of family and friends such as teachers, teaching assistants and sometimes even animals.

CHAPTER 4

Mental Health and Emotional Wellbeing

MILLY

When I met Milly, she was a very sad, anxious, frustrated and angry young woman. I came along after a string of previous clinicians had been involved with her, and she was not amused at having to meet someone new again.

Milly was deceptive, as she presented like a young teenager who was just really annoyed with life and people. Like so many teenagers, you could say; so easy to misinterpret because her presentation could be interpreted as just that, an annoyed teenager, but there was something else. She was aloof and, when she did speak, she had the most superior precise quality to the way she spoke which was not congruent with where she had been brought up in terms of an accent. She had attended a good local school, but the other children spoke with the local accent, as did her sister. This was different. She appeared disinterested, but this could have been because of her previous experiences within services, so there was nothing standing out unless you knew what to look for. Milly was still, not just sitting quietly. She was still. Her face was still. She didn't use gestures, and you couldn't really read what she was thinking or feeling, as there was no reaction apart from an obvious look of disdain when she disagreed with something or didn't like something you had said. Her eye contact was variable and even when prompted in conversation there was no reciprocity. From initial impressions and previous clinical information provided, such as eating difficulties, sleep disturbances, isolating herself and verbal and physical aggressive outbursts, you could easily conclude that Milly was low in mood and look no deeper or, in fact, in a completely different direction. She didn't even show anxiety in the way you would expect to see anxiety present itself. She just appeared disconnected. As time went on it was more evident that the disconnect was actually that, she did not know or have any interest at that time in social etiquette.

The more time I spent with her the clearer it became that she found communicating and interacting difficult. She would become further withdrawn, distant and detached, especially when I tried to explore emotions with her. Milly had found strategies to manage her distress over the years. She had used withdrawal when overload occurred (social and sensory). She used obsessions and rituals to manage and organise her day. She used anger and aggression to clearly communicate to others that she was in distress. She had strategies such as avoidance, absconding, aggression and controlling of others' behaviour and her own eating, but they weren't helping her. They were making her ill and isolating her, as the more she relied on these strategies the more her family found her style of communicating and behaviour challenging. School eventually noticed her withdrawal, but this came after months of educating them in the differences in presentation of young women and because Milly could not sustain masking, as she was physically and emotionally exhausted at this point.

Milly had significant difficulty connecting her emotions to physiological warnings, so emotions would happen to her and then escalate; she was not able to manage the escalation as it was not obvious to her.

Another important element was Milly's sensory issues. The smell of her father's deodorant and aftershave would make her feel ill (although it was generally accepted by most people to be a good smell). Communicating her dislike for something was often a catalyst for a breakdown in relationships, as she would not think twice about how she told a person she didn't like something, often causing distress and upset to the person on the receiving end of Milly's black and white, lacking in empathy, way of explaining something. By the time Milly could communicate her distress, she was already beyond the point of reasoning, hence the outbursts, aggression and absconding. Milly did not understand her triggers and how to modulate or communicate appropriately prior to her arousal levels being out of control. Trying to do work on this with Milly was too hard for her. As a very intelligent young woman she became frustrated with the concept of noticing physical signs of agitation or anxiety or anger in order to control her behaviour. She remained rigid in her belief that if everyone just did what she needed, and did not change things,or expect her to do things she couldn't or didn't want to do, then she would be fine. So, no amount of talking about emotions and managing emotions was working, as Milly was not motivated or able to understand or implement change herself.

The change needed to come from elsewhere. Once we realised this and the pressure was off Milly to change and the onus on others to understand and adapt their behaviour and expectations, then we started to see a shift. Milly's parents and sister worked tirelessly and intensely with me to understand autism. They put their previous upsets and own distress aside and put all their effort into understanding their daughter/sister in the context of autism and how it impacted on her. Lisa would send me reams of incidents, and we would reflect, look for triggers and think about how things could be managed differently. This shift took its toll on the family and the individuals within that family, but they tirelessly sacrificed parts of themselves to ensure they remained supportive, loving parents and sister. They put their trust in me. They took my challenges on board with grace, and they adapted their behaviour. We started to see Milly shift, slowly, but it was there.

What I had to explain to Lisa and Andy was that Milly had had years of being misunderstood, and her behaviour was her way of surviving in a confusing and frustrating world. She was bright enough to know what was going on around her and that she was suffering but unable to communicate for understanding, acceptance and help. Once she and her family knew what 'it' was they could all move forward. With this then came grief. Not for Milly, as she was finally seeing people trying to understand why she thought and did things the way she did, but for Milly's parents and her sister this was a very difficult time as the realisation of the diagnosis became reality and all those years of knowing something was different finally resulted in seeing there was something different... My job then was to enable the grief to move forward and to continue to support through practical advice, honest conversations with all members of the family and strategies to help Milly with her difficulties in executive functioning, rigidity of thought and impact of behaviours on others. This is where the real work began. This is where the real work does begin: the aftermath and fallout after diagnosis. A diagnosis of anything for anyone is traumatic, therefore we need to remember that a diagnosis of an ASC needs aftercare like all other diagnoses would get:

> *Milly*: To me, having Asperger's is just like having brown hair. Having brown hair doesn't define me, it is just something that I was born with, and that I must learn to accept. I can dye my hair a different colour, just like I can put on a 'social mask', but I will always have brown hair underneath.

Milly expands on how she manages her emotional wellbeing daily:

> As an adult, I can now choose the environments that I want to be in, and that has made a huge difference to my outlook on life. When I was younger, I had to do things and go to places where I didn't want to be, but that I had to put up with, and this caused me a lot of anxiety. Now I have control over my own life, and I can choose where I want to go and what I want to do. For me, the main part of having Asperger's is my 'social battery'. I have a certain amount of energy in my battery each week, but by the end of the week most of it will have been used up. I need to recharge it by having some time alone where I can just be myself, but if I don't manage this I end up very stressed and anxious. I also need time to mentally prepare for social occasions. If I know I am going to a party in a couple of weeks, then I am fine, but if I am invited to go somewhere at the last minute, then my anxiety builds up. Being around people in certain environments can take a huge amount of effort. I have no problem with being at work, because I have structure. I know who will be there and what is expected of me, and I have a start and finish time. I feel a lot more comfortable going to work than to a party, where you don't know who will be there or what will happen and there is no specific time you can leave. It is often mentally and physically exhausting being in social situations.

Even though I have got better over the years at picking up social cues and communicating, I can still make mistakes. I have always said exactly what is on my mind, and whilst I have tried to control this as I have got older, I don't always manage it. I also struggle to express myself. If I am talking to someone and I have something to say, I can't always get it out in the right words, or communicate my own thoughts. It is very frustrating to have something you want to say in your head but only something vaguely similar will come out. The biggest strength I have from my Asperger's is my focus and determination. This means that once I start something then I must finish it, and I have a very strong work ethic, but this can also mean I am either all or nothing. If I am concentrating on something and there is an interruption, then it is very hard to move on and do something else as I just can't leave a job half finished, but at the other end of the scale I sometimes won't even attempt something as I know I can't do it to the standard I would like it to be at as a perfectionist. I am very conscientious and sincere, and I am not afraid to stand up for what is right. I am also good at problem solving, and have a good eye for detail. I work with a lot of data, and I can quickly see if there is a mistake or difference in something.

Milly has managed to understand and accept her diagnosis and used her intelligence to use the positives of her Asperger's to her benefit and to acknowledge her difficulties but also to implement strategies to help her manage them within the context of her life.

DARCEY

Darcey was angry and anxious. Her presentation was deceptive. Her eye contact was OK, not exceptionally unusual, perhaps occasionally lacking in modulation, but this could easily be put down to anxiety. She was articulate and forthright. Darcey could eloquently describe situations and scenarios that made her angry and anxious. Darcey's constant lingering anxiety would tend to escalate dramatically into huge episodes of extreme distress, often looking like it had come from nowhere and leaving those around her puzzled at the enormity of her emotional reaction.

What did that really look for me as her clinician, and how was I going to be able to enable her to obtain some emotional understanding, management, resilience and wellbeing?

The main areas which impacted on Darcey's emotional wellbeing were:

- unexpected change

- making her stop what she was doing

- sensory sensitivities such as noise and crowded places

- things not being the way she needed them to be.

I remember Darcey telling me of times when she thought her dad was playing his music too loud, or the base of the music was too deep. Rather than just asking him to turn it down, she would explode into a torrent of physical and verbal outbursts.

Another recurring issue was when her parents would suggest doing something spontaneously together as a family. This could even be something Darcey liked to do, but the spontaneity would cause Darcey to become very rigid and angry, often refusing to do what was asked of her. This would then escalate into a lengthy period of time where she would be very distraught, needing to be left alone but then reassured when she was ready to be reassured. Timing this wrongly was a minefield for Darcey's parents and her sister: the distress would spiral off again.

Darcey was able to let me know what upset her about certain situations but got stuck on others' reactions towards her and their inflexibility. Her sense of injustice about things to do with her was strong, and she would remain upset about things related to this for long periods of time. Darcey's emotions were intense and at times overwhelming and overpowering to her. She has the ability to challenge herself and conquer her anxiety in situations where she is highly motivated to participate, conquering fear of extraordinary levels, but then can be floored by being overwhelmed or unprepared.

Darcey's family was integral in her ability to engage in work with me. Her parents were remarkably supportive and eager for

Darcey to be emotionally well, so that she could achieve her full potential and be happy, and that their family could be the family they wanted it to be. At times things were extremely difficult for them all due to the intensity and frequency of the meltdowns Darcey was having. There was significant strain on them all but they remained supportive and determined to understand and help their daughter/sister. They worked hard in sessions to listen to Darcey's point of view and opinions and remained respectful of her throughout. They gave up work commitments and their own agendas to ensure Darcey had one of them to support her with her appointments at all times. As mentioned previously, Darcey's younger sister Freya was integral in this too, she often had to be brought along to the appointments only to find herself waiting outside the appointment. These displays of support from Darcey's family members gave her visual and emotional evidence that they cared and were investing their own time for her. It also gave me reassurance that the work being done would be implemented and followed up, enhancing the chances for Darcey to achieve her goals of understanding herself and others understanding her.

> *Darcey*: Having Asperger's means a lot to me, as it is part of who I am. I feel that having the label of Asperger's allows me to obtain the help and support I need. It saves time explaining what is wrong and what help I need. At first no teacher in my school knew, which was very frustrating, because it took a long time before I was able to get extra time, etc. Even now that it is more common and most people know what it is, people don't fully understand, and therefore I still find it hard to know what to do to get help. It is important to me, having the label and being given all the facilities to help me which reduces anxiety I may have about exams or other things and the more everyone (including me) learns what it really is and understands it more it will help me and other Aspies to know that we aren't stupid or crazy, but we are all different. I plan to go to university to study psychology. I have always been interested in that area ever since my diagnosis and I find the subject interesting too. As to a career, I'm still undecided, I want to travel and maybe go on to be a clinical psychologist.

ESTHER

Esther was very fragile emotionally but also extremely resilient. She was fragile due to the intensity and frequency of the distress she was experiencing within the school environment. She was having to manage being in a setting which was extremely difficult for her, often ending up in her being isolated due to her perceived anger outbursts or retreating into her own world of selective mutism with limited interactions with anyone.

In order to ensure emotional wellbeing, it was important to find the function/origin of the behaviours/emotions, as although Esther's clinical presentation looked behavioural, the behaviours could have been stemming from social or generalised anxiety in the context of her ASC.

Esther was very black and white in her understanding and emotional presentation. Some of this was her age, and some of it was her cognitive style. Esther had strategies that worked for her, but they were not working in order to help others understand her. They became more of a barrier if not accepted and allowed and understood, as her strategies led her to withdraw and not speak or become angry. For others this was difficult to understand. The inflexibility became obstructive, with the consequence of not being helpful to Esther.

One-to-one talking therapies were not helpful, but concrete evidence for her on how to understand her emotions and manage them were. Being allowed to use what strategies worked for her but with communication to others of the reasons and rationale behind them took the stress out of the expectation to talk and an acceptance that she could use her supportive objects in a more helpful way to all. Once we accepted and understood the impact on Esther's ability to function with these systems in place, things started to move forward. The main barriers for Esther were others not understanding or interpreting her reactions as disrespectful, rude, frustrating and not acceptable. The more these beliefs were expressed and strategies implemented to address these behaviours the more Esther became distressed and fought back. Esther knew she was a good girl. She knew that because she had values and very respectful social networks around her modelling good social etiquette. Her parents parented in the same way, so when she became aware that not only were people not understanding her but labelling her with negative connotations, then it wasn't about caring what others thought of her. It was that what those others thought about why she was presenting as she was, was not true. The injustice of this was palpable when incidents were described to me.

Positive emotional regulation for Esther would mean she would need others to accept and understand her for herself: patience from others. She did not want to change in order to address others' needs, she just wanted to be Esther. Her values were embedded, so her behaviour would change if measures were put in place to accommodate her needs, as this would lower her anxiety and stress and therefore have a positive impact on negative/unhelpful behaviours. Once this was implemented, she began to be able to talk more and trust in those who understood her.

Esther describes how she manages and sees the world around her:

> I do enjoy being a wallflower and watching people run around like chickens without heads a lot and I've found people happy to join me in this activity. Bird watching is also a good pastime, even if it's only seagulls. Apparently, birds are smarter than people.

Esther's mum, Ruth, adds:

> Where are we now. It's not perfect. The high school she is at has good and bad points. I've spent time with the special educational needs coordinator (SENCO) to help them understand Esther, and she has been very supportive and helpful. Most teachers are either excellent and 'get' what she needs or manage to adapt their teaching to her. Other teachers are not so good and want her to comply with how they want things to be rather than what she can cope with.
>
> She has been on school holidays, which are nail-biting times for me. From her last trip, an adventure holiday activity she came back with a certificate for 'best one liners'. She has an extremely dry wit which we all enjoy.

CHAPTER 5

Diagnosis/Labels/ Being Understood

Even though in the current climate we do not subcategorise within the autism spectrum, when these three young women were diagnosed, we did, hence the diagnosis of Asperger's. Currently the average wait for a diagnosis is two years. Girls and young women continue to be underdiagnosed, misdiagnosed and misunderstood. This is not a criticism but an observation. As a clinician still practising I sit alongside colleagues in paediatrics, CAMHS and schools experiencing the continued distress of these young women and seeing the referrals continue to roll in.

Milly: I was in denial about my diagnosis for years. While I knew I was different, I didn't want a label to acknowledge that difference. I had tried so hard to fit in for 14 years and having a label given to me felt like I had failed and the effort I put in had all been pointless. I had managed to conform for so long by watching my peers and putting on an act. Social interaction is not something which came naturally, I worked very hard to appear 'normal' and to say the right things and behave the right way.

Esther: I never cared much about being autistic aside from a few quickly quelled worries. The visits out of school were only a few more in an already long list (allergy clinic, paediatrician) I didn't, and still don't, care if people I barely know don't like me. I have my friends, and I have my family, and I wouldn't change them for the world. Except, maybe my brothers for a new game console. Pretty please? I don't have many friends my own age, as they all care too much about dumb pretty things to me, like make up or the unfair school rules.

Darcey: I was really young when I got diagnosed, so I don't quite remember my exact feelings. I do think I was feeling relieved after the whole process and feeling happy that there was a reason for everything now. I didn't know what autism or Asperger's was, and it opened a whole new world up for me in the fact that there were such things as 'disorders' and 'learning difficulties'. All my life I had questioned why I do things differently than everyone else, why I think the way I do and why I struggle with most things other people find easy. At the age of 12 after everything my case manager Fiona had taught me, I formally presented it back to her, my understanding of autism. Fiona helped in the process of understanding as it was so new to me.

Three very different reactions to the same outcome. This is what as clinicians we need to be aware of. Our pre-diagnosis needs to be vigilant and skilled, and our post-diagnostic work needs to be very individualised and thorough. It is well documented that girls/young women with ASC are deceptive in their clinical presentation; they present emotionally, socially and behaviourally very differently to males.

ADOS scores are often low, if even scoring at all, as they have learnt to mimic and copy social etiquette, enough to get them by socially and in assessments. They have 'enough' reciprocity and social imagination to make you feel you are engaging in social exchanges. Quite a generalisation, but often observed and documented, is that girls often like to read, so are motivated within the parts of the assessment to talk about content of social settings.

Schools will often describe them as shy, focused, driven and passionate. This is in contrast to what parents often see at home which is shutdown, aloof, stubborn, troubled, in distress and challenging. This sounds negative, but due to the energy spent all day from 'fitting in' and 'containing', this is what families experience and witness from their children. These are coping strategies of the individuals themselves to survive. This causes the first confusion, as there is often significant difference in clinical presentation across different settings.

So, for clinicians, the jigsaw pieces rarely fit together as the symptoms are not pervasive across all settings and are not clearly indicative of current diagnostic criteria or research-based assessments such as ADOS.

Girls sometimes manage emotionally by excessive exercise, often interpreted as passion, controlling their dietary intake, often seen as an eating disorder. On the reverse side of this the eating issues are often never investigated as to whether there is a sensory processing or integration difficulty or rigidity and obsessional in nature in the context of their ASC. Extremes of interests are often obsessions, rigidity of thought or rituals. So, when we come to diagnose the picture can be anything but clear.

Stanford University School of Medicine did a research study on 800 children and found gender differences in a core feature of the disorder as well as in the brain structure:

> girls with autism display less repetitive and restricted behaviour than boys. (Supekar and Menon 2015)

The diagnosis is one thing; having a 'label' is another. There is a divide amongst professionals and parents/carers as to the benefit of a label. The only argument I have is that it is very individual. As such this should be explored very early on before any assessment commences.

What I have experienced from some young women prior to diagnosis is their thinking that their difference is something they have done wrong and that they are in some way not worthy and don't fit in, consequently impacting significantly on their emotional wellbeing.

A label is a personal thing but, in the current climate of service provision, there is a need to have a label in order to get the right support and expertise to help. So this adds another layer as, if you don't want the label, you will not get the assessment nor the help. If you accept the label, you are then entitled to the services and help that are available. Also, there is often conflict between children/young people and their parents, who sometimes have differences of opinion as to what would be for the best. Currently parents can choose to obtain a diagnosis, and therefore a label, in the best interests of their children under the age of 16.

Kelly: It was there that our paediatrician recognised in Darcey that she had Asperger syndrome. Fortunately his daughter was also Aspergers, which is how he recognised it. His referral enabled us to succeed in being accepted by CAMHS.

Ultimately the most helpful thing that happened was Darcey's diagnosis. Though this was a long process, by the age of ten Darcey had accepted her condition to be something cherished and became almost 'proud' of it. This acceptance had been part of the way Darcey had been managed by CAMHS and, in particular, had a deep trusting relationship with Fiona. It was also very helpful to us as parents to realise after all this time there had been a mental health issue that had explained the difficulties that we had as a family and with this knowledge gave us even more patience and resilience to support Darcey over the next few years.

Darcey: The main issue for me is the fact that I can hide it well which makes me look normal. When I tell people 'I have Asperger's', every single person says, 'No, you don't', 'Really?', 'You definitely don't'...and that's really frustrating. Everyone has this stereotypical view of what autism is: 'super intelligent, completely unsociable, people like Rainman and Sheldon, good at maths'. All these films and characters and shows based on people with autism just completely set stereotypes to the whole world when it's not always true, and especially most girls with it don't display Sheldon characteristics. Everyone is different, and most people with it are nothing like Rainman. It's so common now, but still no one knows what that can mean, not being able to see the symptoms and effects and how we can be rubbish at maths. It makes me wonder if I even have the disorder when everyone around me assumes I don't have it. It makes me so confused.

Ruth: We had a diagnosis from CAMHS in June 2011. Quite a short journey for us to diagnosis. The first contact from CAMHS came in October 2010, with the first of many forms to fill in and an initial meeting with Fiona and one of her colleagues at which my husband and I agreed for an ASC assessment to be carried out. In December, we had a meeting to consider how CAMHS could support us while we waited for the assessment. In January we received the developmental history report to read through and to check. The first session at CAMHS was with another learning disability nurse. In this Esther named her issue at school 'Stubborn Ben'. We made lists of things Esther was good at, her special powers. I think Esther had a couple of sessions before her diagnosis. First time I realised how focused I was on what Esther couldn't do instead of what she was good at. Probably a result of the interaction with the educational psychologist. In May 2011 we had CAMHS assessing Esther, while I sat behind the one-way glass, and in June we had the diagnosis of autistic spectrum disorder – Asperger syndrome. This time I wasn't relieved. It was an odd feeling. Finally having the official confirmation we needed but there being no 'magic pill' to cure the condition. Normally the doctor works out what is wrong and gives you the medication to fix it. This was lifelong. It probably didn't help that we were having significant difficulties with Esther's school providing any support for her at the time.

Young women in this client group often end up with diagnoses of neuroses, psychoses, OCD, eating disorders, emerging borderline personality disorder, oppositional defiance disorder, anxiety and/or social phobias. So often these still do end up as comorbidities, mainly because of lack of understanding at an early age. Or they remain undiagnosed and untreated/supported. It is crucial that we learn to identify, distinguish and separate symptoms/traits so these long difficult journeys through diagnostic pathways, clinic appointments and so on are limited to appropriate and informative and helpful diagnosis addressing these young women's individualised and specific needs.

Developmental histories need to be detailed, with questions relevant to the most recent information we have on female clinical presentation, remembering that females don't often present with restricted stereotyped behaviours to the same degree as males.

Females are less likely to receive a diagnosis. (Giarelli *et al.* 2010)

With current diagnostic material they may look less autistic, but do not feel and may not be less autistic. (Lai *et al.* 2011)

Prior to assessment collate all previous clinical data about the young person and map the symptoms in a timeline and categorise them. Relevant bits of information can be missed if there have been numerous referrals. It may sound like I'm pointing out the obvious, but these things happen far too often, especially when other professionals work in different trusts.

Look in particular for patterns of symptoms/behaviours which may be explained within an autism context: deteriorations and capacity to cope in adolescence; how transitions were tolerated from nursery to junior to high school; when friendships became difficult.

One of Esther's brothers told his mum that getting Esther diagnosed meant that there was more understanding of him which lead to a diagnosis of ASC for him:

Ruth: Getting Esther's diagnosis meant he got diagnosed.

Darcey's sister Freya writes:

When I was eight, my sister got diagnosed with Asperger syndrome. At the time I didn't know what it was or how it affected her. The way my dad put it was, Darcey struggles to understand people. She finds it hard to see other people's perspective besides her own. For me, this didn't explain the way it made me feel after an argument, or how the little insignificant things made Darcey angry. It didn't explain why I couldn't tell my friends or why I had always had to be the bigger person. You never get used to coping with someone with Asperger's no matter how many times you go through the same arguments over and over again. Even now, I still have to be reminded of it. It's not her fault. Now, when I try and explain to people how this syndrome affects my sister, people find it hard to understand. The common responses are things like, 'but she looks normal' or 'maybe she is just shy'. Even I struggle to get into my head exactly what Asperger's is, because it is hard to distinguish what is Asperger's and what is my sister. I used to always get so angry with my parents for dismissing Darcey's abusive behaviour, as though when she acted out, it was okay. I remember thinking, 'What if that's just Darcey getting what she wants?' Selfish as it seemed, it's what I felt quite a lot. However, there were times when Darcey was just Darcey. When we would argue, she would always slip a letter under my door explaining exactly how she felt and how sorry she was I had to put up with her. It was how she would communicate with me, through writing. Every letter I kept because it reminded me of how she felt. My dad used to say that living with Darcey can be strength. She has taught me to have patience with people, to be supportive and to be strong.

Whilst supporting our young women, we need to promote how different we all are and how differently we all think and that all of these ways are important and valued.

CHAPTER 6

Comorbidities

There are numerous comorbidities which are often the primary diagnosis initially for a lot of our young women. I will be looking at those most often encountered by clinicians, particularly at referral and initial assessment, as it is here that appropriate pathways and treatment/interventions are determined.

This is not a chapter to teach you about the different diagnoses, merely an explanation of what the most common ones associated or missed or misdiagnosed are within ASC, so you can be more aware when the clinical presentation is complex.

SELECTIVE MUTISM

Selective mutism is thought to be triggered by severe social anxiety. What you actually see is the young person being affected by the inability to construct words. Their physiological sensations take over, and this can cause tension, obstructing the airway, which in turn impacts on their breathing. They often experience palpitations which leave them immobile and in pain and frightened. They will often respond to this 'panic' by running or freezing or becoming angry (fright, flight and freeze), and their processing can also be affected. Selective mutism has been described by some young people as their brain not working in words but in images, sounds and patterns. Andi says,

> I have a difficult time speaking fluently as it is because my brain doesn't work in words. It works in images, sounds and patterns. (Simone 2010, p.72)

I have seen this numerous times when young women are significantly anxious; it's like their whole translation/communication system breaks down and getting the thoughts and feelings from their head to their mouths to speak or hands to write or type is impossible. This level of anxiety often originates from social anxiety and significant lack of confidence and trust in others to understand them.

The difference between this being a standalone diagnosis or an additional trait to ASC is in the evidence of where the mutism occurs. Often, when this is not related to autism, the individual is able to speak and interact normally in all other settings other than the ones which increase anxiety, particularly social settings, so observation of the young person in all settings is crucial in order to understand its origin. Also behaviours not indicative of ASC need to be observed.

Milly exhibited not speaking from time to time; the main times she would default to this were in situations that were very challenging and anxiety-provoking to her, for example, social settings, being with unfamiliar people, feeling overwhelmed by her emotions and when she was challenged about expressing her emotions. At this point it was questioned whether this was mutism and/or alexithymia.

On four occasions within my career I have come across the link between subclinical seizures and mutism. I know this is infrequent in the context of the number of young women and the 32 years I have worked within this client group, but it warrants a mention as:

> Subclinical seizures could be the possible cause of underlying mutism. (Simone 2010, p.72)

Don't be averse to asking paediatricians' advice. Make sure you have evidence for them to be able to justify further medical investigations. Just because the numbers are minimal does not mean they are not worthy of further investigation/exploration. The more we rule out the more likely we are to discover what we are actually dealing with.

EATING DISORDERS

Recent research indicates that the percentage of young women with ASC and an eating disorder has increased. The University of Cambridge in 2013 studied girls with eating disorders and ASC. This revealed that females with anorexia have elevated autistic traits (Baron-Cohen *et al.* 2013).

> Emerging research shows that people with eithers condition have difficulties understanding and interpreting social cues, and tend to fixate on tiny details that make it difficult to see the big picture. What's more, both groups of people often crave rules, routines and rituals. Genetic studies also suggest overlaps between autism and anorexia. (Arnold 2016)

Milly

Milly experienced difficulties with eating at different stages of her childhood and early adolescence.

> *Milly*: I have always had a complicated relationship with food. When I was younger, I found many foods overpowering in both taste and texture, and would endeavour to only eat bland meals. I avoided trying new foods at all costs, and still have some sensory issues with food now. I can't bear the sound of people eating certain foods such as cereal or other crunchy foods, and I often found it excruciating. I also find the smell of some food overwhelming, and was once found emptying the untouched contents of my lunchbox into a bin at school, as to me, the smell of my lunchbox was unbearable. Mealtimes were a constant battle against my parents, who would attempt to encourage me to increase my limited repertoire, but being forced to try new foods was an extremely distressing event and even the thought of having to put something unfamiliar in my mouth was anxiety inducing. I would try to have things as plain as possible, with no extra sauce or dressing, as it was just too many flavours for me to cope with at once.
>
> Even now I am older, I am still quite sensitive to food, and find foods with certain textures intolerable, but I now have a

much less restricted diet. However, I still prefer meals separated into different components rather than all being mixed together on my plate, as I can eat one thing at a time and anticipate each taste and texture before I eat it. The whole premise of mealtimes as a child was stressful, as although I would ask every day what we would be having for dinner, I wouldn't always get an answer, and so many meals came as an unpleasant surprise. Not knowing what I was going to get until I sat down at the table was very difficult, as it gave me no time to mentally prepare for the food. This is still important to me, and so whilst it doesn't affect me to the extent that it used to, I will still never go to a restaurant without looking at the menu in advance. I saw food as a fuel – something that was necessary but I could gain no pleasure from, and there were very few foods that I would actually enjoy eating. I had no appetite and attempts to introduce new foods into my diet were futile. I would have gladly had the same few meals every week, and I had no desire to try anything else, as, in my mind, once I had a few foods that I found acceptable then why should I bother trying anymore? I was also a very slow eater, and so would often find myself in uncomfortable situations. I was almost always last to finish in the dining hall at school, and so on several occasions I was left there by myself, making it even harder as all the focus then shifted on to the food in front of me. As a child, food was one of the few things in my life I could control, and so I would take it to the extreme and would often find an excuse to skip meals. I was also repeatedly found sitting in the kitchen what seemed like several hours after a mealtime had started, as I just couldn't bring myself to put what was in front of me in my mouth. I still have the occasional issue but, now I am older, I have a much wider range of foods that I find acceptable.

Lisa: At bedtimes Andy and I had to regularly remove food from her cheeks that she secreted in them rather than swallow. Mostly it was meat or fish that she had chewed until it was a matted lump. She was a hamster.

Lisa: In our opinion, whilst she is relatively inactive she still appears to consume too little food and has a controlling attitude towards it, i.e. preferring an apple to lunch or just skipping meals altogether. She is very aware of what constitutes healthy eating and tends to refuse anything she considers 'full of sugar' or too filling, i.e. rice, potatoes.

The triggers for Milly appeared to be a combination of anxiety, sensitivities and control and these times were incredibly distressing for Milly and her parents. However, Milly has now over time found her own ways of managing her relationship with food.

I think it is important to note that there need to be clinicians who are skilled in seeing the traits of ASC and confident and skilled to work in these teams. Working in different ways can consequently improve outcomes for this percentage of young women who find themselves in eating disorder services, but if managed and understood differently may be able to develop a different and more helpful relationship with food. If this is not addressed in an ASC way, then the outcomes can be tragic, as you are working against their difference in a way that does not fit.

Esther

Ruth: Esther has food sensitivity and likes the same meal plan every week unless she instigates the change. She has got better as she used to only be able to eat only Tesco rolls, not any other brand of roll, and now she can, but she can still taste the difference. She can tell the difference between dad cooking a dish and mum.

What needs to be considered is what the driver is behind the restricted eating and what interventions are most appropriate. It may be that traditional and current therapies used in eating disorders may be difficult for young people on the spectrum to understand and implement, as understanding their own feelings, the impact of their behaviour on others and others' feelings is core to their difficulties. These skills need to be present in the eating disorder teams.

Darcey

Darcey: I was and still am a fussy eater. I cannot eat anything someone has touched or picked up from their fork instead of mine. I can't eat food if it looks funny or is on a dirty looking plate. Same applies to drinks, I can't drink from the same cup or liquid as someone else might have sipped and put saliva back into the drink. Once I've eaten something in a certain format, e.g. sweet potato mash, I can't eat it another way, e.g. sweet potato chips. I also can't chew certain foods together depending on their texture, e.g. hard peas with mash because it feels weird to chew but that's not that often.

Finally, on eating, my boyfriend reminded me that I'm still funny with food regarding the order in which I eat something... putting the milk in first, and then cereal bit by bit, and then maybe adding more of it. I only eat for fuel rather than pleasure, but I was always lucky that my mum was a great cook and a lot of the time, specialised most meals around what I liked. I tend to only eat the same snack until I hate it, such as Aero mint chocolate, and wouldn't eat any other chocolate, as there was no point if I'd already found a favourite food. I also usually only eat the same meal at any pub which is a tuna melt baguette, so my dad always has to ask the bar if they can specially make it and, if not, I sometimes refuse to eat anything else on the menu.

Kelly: My own recollection of Darcey and her eating habits was that she was a nightmare as a baby and hardly ate. Mealtimes were more like a circus act, constant entertaining or distracting to get food inside her. Also, everything had to be warm, never cold and, although she was breastfed, it had to be with nipple shields else she wouldn't feed.

ADHD

A combination or overlapping of developmental disorders such as attention deficit hyperactivity disorder (ADHD) and ASC will most definitely increase the severity of the symptoms. If you combine difficulties with social communication and interaction, rigidity of thought and imagination and then add additional difficulties such as lack of focus, hyperactivity and impulse control, then what you see is an increase in externalising and/or internalising emotion which in turn manifests in all social contexts. These difficulties will impact on cognitive and social functioning.

Children and young people with these complex constellations of difficulties are becoming more and more common in our appointments. As clinicians, we need to be aware that such complexities exist and acknowledge the risk that comes with this combination of the two conditions. We will need to consider how we assess and manage the difficulties these young people present with, as the interventions we offer will need to address the complexity.

In terms of diagnosis, the *Diagnostic and Statistical Manual of Mental Disorders* (American Psychiatric Association 2013; DSM-5) states that you can be diagnosed with different diagnoses running alongside one another. When the criteria are met for both disorders, both diagnoses are given. There is an essential need for more research to identify the behavioural characteristics of girls and young women with co-occurring ASC and ADHD so that specialised interventions can be appropriately implemented to improve outcomes and quality of life for this cohort. Ultimately, though, we need to remember that ADHD can also look different in girls and sometimes emotional dysregulation or sensory processing difficulties look very like ADHD.

Colombi and Ghaziuddin (2017, p.1) describe the comorbidities as impacting on 'increased anxiety, worse working memory, and less empathy', which emphasises the increased challenges individuals with both diagnoses face and highlights the need for specialist assessment and intervention.

Mental health difficulties feature significantly in this group of individuals as diagnosis, services, interventions and understanding is often lacking, limited or non-existent.

PSYCHOSIS

This is certainly a complex topic, and one area which requires specialists in both areas, of ASC and mental health, in order to assess, monitor and ensure the right advice and pathway are offered. Many referrals that are received of young women with ASC state that the young woman is hearing voices. There are important differences between hearing external voices and our internal dialogue, but sometimes the way our young women express, experience and report what they hear makes it difficult to know what they are actually experiencing. The difference in ways of thinking, sensory processing differences and significant anxiety can sometimes manifest like a psychotic episode but can also actually turn into a psychotic episode if not recognised and/or treated.

None of the three young women we have been discussing experienced psychosis, but other young women I have worked with have. Most of those had been under significant and prolonged amounts of stress related to the difficulties they were having from the impact of their autism, the lack of understanding they received and their specific individual needs. Lack of sleep, lack of food and fluids also contributed to these episodes. Therefore, management of anxiety therapeutically is crucial and sometimes medication is required. This may be in the form of melatonin to aid sleep or an anti-anxiolytic, antidepressant and/or an antipsychotic to enable a calmer state of mind and physical equilibrium so the individual can access talking or other forms of psychological therapies, exercise or hobbies which enable emotional wellbeing.

Here is an example of how a young woman found a different way of working out an emotional connection with herself, but that if misunderstood or looked at from a different clinical perspective could have been managed in a way that could have had detrimental outcomes. She devised different characters to represent different parts of her personality. They all had names and when she spoke of them she explained that they spoke with each other and they were in control of her. The descriptions were elaborate and detailed and, on first hearing, concerning, especially when she described some of the characters as 'the sociopath and the psychopath'. You can see how this warranted further exploration; it was eventually explained within the context of ASC, but it could have been accounted for as a psychotic episode and the pathway and outcome for her could have been catastrophic. Much depended on the skills of the clinicians layering down the origin of the thought process, so when investigated further, it was found that this was the young woman's way of understanding herself. What led on from this was an understanding that these parts of her were also representations of her emotions. Eventually, once she had worked this out, with support from me and supervision from psychology, she was able to move fully to being able to recognise the emotions and became empowered to manage them. The characters were, for her, halfway to understanding why she thought, felt and acted as she did. This stage enabled her to acknowledge and accept that we all have different sides to our personalities and that that is OK, and that each of those sides often emerge when driven by emotion. What was fundamental in her understanding was that she was in control of those other parts of her and the emotions that were driving them, and even the characters she didn't like were eventually normalised and accepted as OK and managed in a more helpful way to her. She began to see their function and that sometimes these were survival/protective factors. This was done by social storying and using examples of emotions and linking them to characteristics of the personalities. What was leading to her significant distress was the feeling of being out of control. Once she owned and managed the different sides of her she became less anxious and more accepting and understanding of herself.

DIFFICULTIES WITH PROCESSING AND MODULATING RESPONSES TO SENSATIONS

This is an area that needs accurate assessment and understanding within the context of the complexities of these young women. Difficulties with sensory integration and processing can impact on the ability to tolerate certain situations, which in turn can impact on self-esteem and confidence, anxiety and low mood and vice versa. If you are anxious, you are more likely to be hypervigilant, particularly with sight and sound. Differentiating between the potential causations for emotional dysregulation is vital (if possible to define), as the way this is approached clinically is very different.

Esther: I hate crowds with a passion, but so long as I'm with someone I can deal with being in one. I enjoy it because then we can complain about people doing silly things together. And, by crowds, I mean any place housing six or more people. Like the hell on earth, supermarkets.

Darcey: I can just about cope with crowded noisy places for so long, such as parties or busy streets. At first I am okay with it all, but within an hour I become very distressed, anxious and mostly angry leading to pushing people (usually at parties) who bump into me, or I start to cry and yell how I feel, which is usually only when my parents are around. At parties, after a certain amount of time, the noises and lights become heightened and result in me becoming upset and needing to get out.

All three young women experienced sensory processing integration difficulties and these are described throughout. Again these difficulties can manifest themselves in all sorts of different ways, not just the documented stereotypical ways, so be vigilant and question.

SOCIAL ANXIETY

The DSM-5 (American Psychiatric Association 2013) talks about social anxiety as being in a state of continual worry, pervasive across all areas of a person's life, when in situations of unfamiliarity, these being either settings and/or people. And the worry of their intense reactions or overwhelming feelings during this time causes their behaviour and/or communication to be perceived by others as extreme or unusual, resulting in them feeling embarrassed.

It is important to understand the reasons for the social anxiety and to appreciate and support appropriate management strategies. For young women on the spectrum social anxiety is often reported to be more about anxiety about the expectation of reciprocal conversation, the unexpected elements of a conversation potentially with someone they don't know, making mistakes or them perceived as making mistakes, not knowing what to do if they start to find things difficult, the number and kind of people who will be there and new people within a new situation – finding the whole social communication and interaction experience exhausting emotionally and physically.

Supporting and enabling our young women to manage these situations in a more helpful way to them needs to include practice and positive experiences. One strategy which is still advised as a frontline intervention is a social communication group. However, be mindful, as although this may seem like a good idea and may work for some, it needs to be thought about on an individual basis. I say this, as I have never been so humbled as when a young woman spoke candidly to me:

> Why on earth would you send me to a group which will heighten my anxiety, to then share the space with other anxious individuals, all of us struggling with social communication difficulties and then have to act and be expected to be able to do that in a different place that we are unfamiliar with?

I've never forgotten these words, and I often think of them when services give this as the only option for an intervention, and when young people aren't able to access it they are discharged as seen as not engaging and rarely offered other interventions.

GENERALISED ANXIETY

Anxiety can manifest itself in so many ways and can be very individualised. We regularly see behavioural presentations that, when explored, stem from anxiety and that often mask themselves as anger. Anxiety impacts on sleep, appetite, relationships, everyday functioning and learning.

If in the case of our young women it is seen as a standalone issue, the way it is approached clinically with the individual may be unhelpful and at times detrimental, the reason being that if the generalised anxiety is not understood in the context of the complexity of an individual with ASC then the strategies employed may be unsustainable.

OBSESSIVE COMPULSIVE DISORDER

In the context of a comorbidity to ASC then the function and origin of OCD needs to be understood. There is some similarity between OCD behaviour and the behaviours we see in ASC as repetitive and or ritualistic. What seems to separate the two is that:

> In ASC the children are not likely to obsess about their rituals and are more likely to simply act on their urges...they may present with limited insight into the reason behind their ritualized behaviours... they are less likely to be using their ritualized behaviours to neutralise fear or anxiety and or keep bad things from happening, as would be true for OCD. (Montague and Rastall 2013)

What we need to be looking out for and aware of is:

> ASC ritualized behaviours may be satisfying other needs such as modifying sensory input, gaining reinforcement from the environment or preserving sameness in their everyday lives. (Montague and Rastall 2013)

How you then support with appropriate strategies is crucial, as you would tackle these in very different ways. So, in terms of ASC, you would think about sensory assessments and strategies to manage sensory needs and/or timetables, helpful routines and planning for unexpected change with things like Social Stories™ and reflection on situations that were unexpected but that were managed, examining how the situation was manageable, drawing on strengths and experiences to rewrite difficult experiences with unexpected change.

SELF-HARM AND SELF-INJURY

An act with a non-fatal outcome, in which an individual deliberately initiates a non-habitual behaviour that without intervention from others will cause self-harm.

> Self-injury is highly prevalent in children and adolescents with ASC. Atypical sensory processing and the need for sameness were contributors to self-injury, indicating that clinicians may

want to focus on these two risk factors to develop function-based treatments for self-injury. (Duerden *et al.* 2012)

There are four categories to self-harm/self-injury that Simeon and Favazza (2001, p.2) list:

- stereotypic
- major
- compulsive
- impulsive.

And there are various forms of self-harm:

- cutting
- stabbing
- scratching the skin
- placing sharp objects under the skin
- biting the inside of the mouth
- picking at sores and reopening wounds
- burning the skin with heat or chemicals
- pulling hair out
- bruising or breaking bones by hitting
- using ligatures to restrict blood flow
- ingesting toxins or objects.

Forms of self-harm can be to the:

- arms and wrists
- legs
- abdomen
- head
- chest and breasts
- genitals.

What you might also see is:

- head banging

- pulling eyelashes

- restricting eating

- piercings

- tattoos

- excessive exercising.

Self-harm from my experience is often a communication of significant distress, past, present or both. Children with high functioning ASC may deliberately self-harm as a way of coping with anxiety and feelings of being different. So, what we need to look at is the individuals understanding emotions, learning to manage and appropriately regulate them and finding ways to communicate their distress or confusion in ways that are less harmful and more helpful to them.

LEARNING DIFFICULTIES

In the UK, the term 'learning difficulty' includes children and young people who have 'specific learning difficulties', for example, dyslexia, but who do not have a significant general impairment of intelligence. This is often seen in our young people with ASC in the forms of dyslexia and dyscalculia.

Darcey was never diagnosed with dyslexia, but we did an experiment one day with colours of background paper and different colours of pens to check which combinations worked better for her as she had been expressing difficulties with the glare of whiteboards and white paper. This led to Darcey using overlays at school and her school acknowledging that she needed support in this area.

This came from an awareness of Irlen syndrome, which I had seen with a couple of my other children with ASC. Seven years or so ago, though, Irlen's wasn't as well known as it is now.

Irlen Syndrome (also referred to at times as Meares-Irlen Syndrome, Scotopic Sensitivity Syndrome, and Visual Stress) is a perceptual processing disorder. It is not an optical problem. It is a problem with the brain's ability to process visual information. This problem tends to run in families and is not currently identified by other standardized educational or medical tests. (Irlen 2017)

Since Darcey gave me insight into these difficulties I regularly play the paper and pens game. Often the results are staggering, warranting me to communicate with schools to implement the use of overlays and different screen covers. These things may sound simple, but to young people experiencing sensory integration difficulties it can impact hugely on their learning and their physical wellbeing.

This is not a standardised test but a clinician using knowledge and thinking out of the box to support the emotional wellbeing of their young person. In itself it's simple, but it can lead to a more in-depth assessment and further layered understanding of that individual.

LEARNING DISABILITIES

A learning disability in the UK is currently described as 'arrested or incomplete' growth of the mind during the early stages of development which can impact on the overall level of functioning. It is important to stress however, that each country has its own terminology, for example, intellectual disability or individuals who are intellectually challenged.

I won't elaborate on this area as the focus is on the young women in this book who all had diagnoses of Asperger's, so do not have a learning disability, but it needs a mention for those girls and young women who do.

DEPRESSION

The prevalence of childhood depression has been estimated to be 1 per cent in pre-pubertal children and around 3 per cent in post-pubertal young people. It is experienced by twice as many adolescent females as males (NICE 2017).

Many women with autism I have worked with describe themselves as being depressed forever, and say that their low mood is a consequence of their limited social acceptance and daily challenges; they are unable to differentiate their depression from their autism. Problems with identifying emotional responses (alexithymia) from physical sensations can form part of this difficulty as they may not actually know how they are feeling or be able to articulate that into words. I also wonder whether having lived with a constant sense of low mood and stress for most of one's life results in not actually knowing what OK feels like (Hendrickx 2015).

Darcey, Milly and Esther all presented with low mood, but it manifested itself in different ways: eating issues, anger, anxiety and obsessional thinking. It was hard to know at times what was impacting on what. What I can advise is that through assessing, observing and formulating you can start to find practical ways to alleviate some of the symptoms mentioned previously, which will then impact on low mood; vice versa, if you are able to get the low mood under effective management, then the other symptoms will decrease. Sometimes it's just trial and error. Often the best way is to work with what is distressing and impacting on the young person the most as they will be more motivated to change that element; then you can measure the improvement and adapt your therapy/interventions accordingly. This is where your expertise really kicks in, not just accepting initial clinical presentations and referring to the pathway relevant to that presentation. Look in depth and from different angles, assess holistically, as this will give you a more informed decision pathway, reducing too many changes for the young person within the service and getting the right pathway from the onset.

SLEEP DISORDERS

Sleep problems are very common within ASC. Lack of sleep or productive sleep can result in daytime sleepiness, learning problems and behavioural issues such as hyperactivity, inattentiveness and aggression; these I see regularly with my young women.

Sleep problems can be divided into:

- Settling problems, where a child has difficulty going to sleep.

- Waking problems, where a child wakes repeatedly during the night.

A combination of the above is also very common.

- 'Social cueing' problems, where your child doesn't make the connection between the family going to bed and their own need to sleep.

- Melatonin issues which can be identified by deficits in hormonal regulation or actual production of the right amount at the right time, additionally impacted upon by sleep routines not implemented in the child's/young person's life.

- Sensory issues.

- Problems caused by allergy and food sensitivities.

- Hypersomnia – sleeping too much and sleep–wake reversal.

All three young women experienced difficulties with sleep.

Lisa describes Milly as a youngster 'always waking up screaming'. Lisa sought advice from the health visitor who suggested that when Milly woke she should say, 'I've had a lovely sleep'. Lisa goes on to remember:

From that day on Milly awoke repeating those exact words verbatim at the top of her voice *every* morning without fail for months. It was only marginally better than her screaming. She never slept during the day even as a young baby, too fearful that she would miss something, but she did sleep well at night.

Ruth describes the following:

Esther finds sleeping hard and currently records how often she wakes in the night, which is numerous times. Esther also finds one of the bedrooms in her house too quiet to sleep.

Darcey: I struggled to sleep when I was little, because I was constantly thinking or wide awake, so my parents would usually tell me stories or do relaxation techniques to put me to sleep. Regarding the sleeping now, I don't notice it as much as then because I am older and go to bed later, so I sleep when I'm actually tired. But when I was younger, I used to want to stay up late, or when I'd go to bed, I'd stay up learning lyrics or singing due to not falling asleep.

GENDER ISSUES

This is such a complex topic that all I would like to comment on here is that if you are in a position of discussing and supporting one of your girls/young women, focus on identity and not gender initially. From an understanding of one's own identity comes self-esteem and self-confidence which then equips resilience within future conversations around gender.

CHAPTER 7

Assessments

We all, as professionals and clinicians, have guidelines, guidance and expectations that we have to adhere to which are based on evidence and research. However, we are working and building relationships with individuals who are complex and need understanding, nurturing and encouragement to be the best they can be, so our guidance needs to be flexible within the boundaries of the assessments.

We expect these *unique* developing young women to fit into boxes in respect of labels and therapy, which we now know (through experience and research) often don't fit their different ways of thinking or represent their actual adversities. This makes it confusing for us and them as to how to proceed and make the assessments as appropriate, meaningful and helpful to them whilst giving us the information we need to mould our interventions to their need.

So as clinicians what do we do when:

- *we* are confused

- *we* are stuck

- *we* are bound by our clinical and professional bodies and management structures and service provision to use certain pathways?

It's not just the young people who get stuck. We get stuck too, and what is helpful when this happens is to step back, reflect, review, re-evaluate, modify and adjust. Ask for help, look out of the box, reformulate. This is important when faced with working with young women experiencing difficulties with assessment processes and with the outcome potentially being a label or diagnosis which they see as something alien to them. This, in turn, will therefore impact on their understanding and acceptance of it and potentially impact on their emotional wellbeing, as sometimes their main driver is to manage so they are not seen as different. They have so often blended in, becoming chameleons, camouflaging themselves to adapt to the situations they are faced with.

The way assessments are delivered and executed needs careful consideration.

> The team conducting the assessment needs to be a specialist age appropriate integrated autism team and should be part of a part of a local autism diagnostic pathway. (Autism Act 2009)

The assessments *are* evolving, but this takes time. So, whilst we wait for our revised versions/adaptations, which will hopefully represent and focus on the differences of young women's clinical presentation, helping to understand and identify their ability to mask and play the social game, it is essential that we peel back their layers of complexity and challenge our clinical skills and prejudices within the current frameworks. We need to be research savvy and skilled in our observational skills and interpretation of responses and behaviours.

During your assessments, wherever they may be or whatever format they take, consider the following: assessments do not have to just rely on sitting in a clinic room answering questions. Assessments can be done anywhere and in any form. You just need to adapt the assessment to the individual. If it is the requirement of the assessment to sit in a room, remember to incorporate all your knowledge on that young person to make the experience as comfortable and helpful as possible, taking into account any specific individual needs they may have.

Ensure you take a thorough developmental history with the depth of knowledge incorporating, for instance, questions about how the young person as a baby transitioned from breast/bottle to milk. Did they gag at all when they transitioned onto solid food? Did they share eye contact with you when you fed them?

In 2008, Chawarska, Klin and Volkmar published their research into social development in babies and the importance of noticing babies with difficulties with social resonance. They talk about the first two years of life as a window of opportunity to intervene.

They used eye-tracking to learn about social engagement and how newborns engage with the world. They found that children without autism look at emotional reactions, and children with potential autism look at the things that are moving around them. Therefore, early identification is possible within the first six months before behaviours set in. Thus they recommend the need for universal treatment in the early years. Their intent is to ensure that individuals reach their potential but retain their identity as we need their diversity.

Make sure you really understand the maternal and paternal lines. Get the parents of your children to describe their relatives and themselves in depth. Often people miss out crucial bits of information because we have not asked the right question, we have not built on information offered or we haven't delved deep enough. Don't be afraid to dig. Developmental histories are imperative, as are observations in all settings, so we can start to identify appropriately whether the behaviours being presented are based on issues connected with reciprocal social interaction and communication and repetitive activities and narrow interests. Dig deep and wide with your questions in the developmental history, investigate the family tree, recognise traits which are described as 'quirky', 'aloof', 'disorganised', 'class clown', 'shy'. Notice any comments about anyone excelling at anything or, on the contrary, struggling, or about individuals with eccentricities, obsessions or routine orientation. Look for patterns in the lineage.

Try to observe the young woman prior to commencing the assessment. Don't get distracted with previous descriptions of shyness, appropriate social skills, descriptions of an introvert. Be curious. What do these portrayals look like in your young woman?

- Look at their interests with a more critical eye. How intense are they? How much do they dominate conversation or mould their social interactions? Are they copied?

- Observe their interactions. Do they watch? Do they stay on the periphery of social situations? Do they seem natural and at ease? Do they take control of the situation and dominate?

- Do they read those complex situations and modulate their behaviours and adapt and adjust? Do they overcompensate or detach? Do they move around in order to avoid those difficult social interactions, concealing their anxieties and awkwardness?

- Don't dismiss or accept previous diagnoses of OCD, self-harm and eating disorders. Instead question how these presented. Look for triggers, patterns in behaviour. Look at the function behind the behaviours and the contexts. Explore whether there is a correlation in increase in frequency or intensity when in social settings or within relationships.

- Look at the area of repetitive behaviour and special interests, as these often get missed as OCD or just 'something girls do' and the interests are 'normal girls' interests'. It's the characteristics and the intensity and depth of that interest that matter.

- Monitor anxiety. Watch if it changes when obsessions and motivators are withdrawn or not paid attention to.

- Scrutinise when change is implemented, when change is unexpected or when demands are placed on them.

- Observe the impact of their sensory world being compromised.

- Watch the reactions when conversations are not including their interests or the conversations become emotive.

- Look for motivators and passions/obsessions.

- Don't expect individuals to fit into a box or a system, don't make young women look at you or put their hoods down or stop them taking their shoes off or moving around.

- Give them as much opportunity for us to see them as them and in order to see this we need to see them at their most relaxed as well as at their most challenged.

Use your experience, your clinical expertise and your instinct to work in an individualised way. You *will* need to think out of the box.

- You may need go to their home. You may need to go for a walk with their dogs. You may need to paint nails together or draw or interact through technology such as messaging or emailing whilst in the same room.

- Watch for changes in body language and eye contact.

- Sometimes you may think you see and hear that they have empathy, some imagination and some theory of mind and sense of humour. Check it out, dig deep, make sure what you are seeing and hearing is not learnt and rehearsed.

- Don't be misled into thinking that if your young woman shows appropriate skills of one-to-one interaction with you that that is a measure of her actual ability. This can be a learned behaviour within that interaction type. This would need further observations within many settings across various relationship types to measure the accuracy and outcomes.

- Keep up to date with research and acknowledge the parameters of current assessments in terms of their preference towards the male brain theory.

- Ensure you have a clear indication of their cognitive profile.

- Check how they function with friendships and whether they are organised by their parents or not.

If it's there, and you know what you are looking for and you have the skill to tease it out, you will see it. It is hard to mask something when the person scrutinising you knows what they are scrutinising and has skills to execute the assessment effectively to get the right information to inform the process and ultimately the diagnosis.

As with all diagnostic tools and criteria remember to look beyond the assessment but within the young women, as you will need to be astute to recognise the complex, diverse and hidden difficulties.

Current questionnaires can be difficult for parents and teachers to know how to answer correctly so check the questions have been understood. Acknowledge if parents may have any literacy or social communication difficulties themselves. Be mindful of their insight and understanding of not only the questionnaires and the words but also the inference.

So often, if you just ask, 'Does anyone have any learning difficulties, disabilities, mental health difficulties?', people will say no, but if you ask about being shy or disorganised or not liking school you may get a different answer. You can always be true to the original question, but adapting the language may support the person answering the questions to give you an honest answer rather than guessing at one.

Consistency of questionnaires and relevance are important. So many different ones are used which does muddy the waters somewhat. Current questionnaires are geared towards the male brain, and one difference that is presented in girls is the part of the triad which describes repetitive and narrow interests. These questions are often misinterpreted or just dismissed, as the nature of the interest may be seen as being within the norm for other girls. The difference is that the topic/type is often something you would recognise girls having an interest in and, with something like reading particular things, it would be put down to a studious intelligent girl, not a girl with an increased interest in a repetitive behaviour. This is where clinical skill and understanding are so important otherwise we fall at the first hurdle.

We need to be attentive to assessments being outdated and needing revision to ensure the girls and young women are represented clinically accurately. Studies are underway to look at adapting the current diagnostic tools and a team of Australian scientists along with a Polish scientist is looking at a questionnaire specifically for girls, the Q-ASC, the questionnaire for autism spectrum conditions (Attwood, Garnett and Rynkiewicz 2016).

Each assessment is vital in the understanding of the individual seeking answers to why they are experiencing difficulties and/or distress. So don't be too rigid, think carefully about how you present the questions and be aware of any communication difficulties your reporters may have.

In clinical settings and in teams of clinicians it is imperative that the style and type of assessments are appropriate to client need. Ensure your assessments complement each other. Think about the core difficulties and if you think you need more evidence to support an appropriate diagnosis liaise with your colleagues. Additional information may be the difference between a diagnosis or not. The impact on the individual and the time aspect of waiting for further assessments to inform the process may affect their resilience to manage and consequentially they may experience emotional dysregulation. This continues to happen in clinical practice, particularly with girls/young women. The standardised tests are completed but often there are discrepancies between school and home questionnaires, school do not see/report/ understand the difficulties yet home reports significant difficulties, developmental histories are inconclusive, often school and home observations are not completed so information is sparse. ADOS is not offered regularly and, even when it is, girls often don't score as clinicians stick rigidly to the format and do not check and 'layer down' as I call it, particularly within the areas related to reciprocity.

It is imperative you check reciprocity, as many girls/young women have learned to answer questions and ask one back, and they can also engage in reciprocity when they are interested in something you are talking about or when you show interest in their interest or motivation. Switch to something out of their comfort zone or interest area and then you will see whether there is a difficulty with reciprocity. Current ADOS and deliverance of ADOS does not lend itself well to this.

Darcey was deceptive as she was articulate. Her eye contact was well modulated, and she could report what caused her distress. What stood out was the significant difficulties with reciprocal social interaction and communication. It wasn't how she spoke. There were no obvious intonation or stereotypical traits there, but it was what she said about what happened to her on a daily basis when she was interacting with others and the repetitiveness of the amount and types of misunderstandings, rigidities and significant emphasis from her around injustices. It wasn't her behaviour in clinic or the reported anger and anxiety reported by Kelly and Ashley that alerted us, but how Darcey herself reported events within friendships and repeated difficulties with understanding others and social contexts. If the skills of the clinicians hadn't been attuned to these difficulties and what that might represent, she would have been sent down a route of anxiety and anger management.

Once we had an idea that Darcey may be experiencing difficulties with social communication and rigidity of thought, we could have conversations with her and her parents as to the best route to take in order to get Darcey to understand why she was having difficult experiences. So instead of seeing anger and anxiety as the primary drivers for her behavioural presentation, we saw them as functions of communicating her distress at thinking differently and being misunderstood and her misunderstanding others.

I hope you can see the different directions you can take as clinicians and professionals and the different clinical and educational pathways you can choose dependent on what you think the driver/function of the clinical presentation is. I hope you can also see, therefore, how wrong we can be and how unhelpful our interventions can potentially be.

Milly too had been misunderstood. She and her parents have described how difficult the process of getting to the appropriate clinical team/practitioner was. Milly had her ADOS at home. She was prepared prior to myself and the other ADOS examiner turning up to her house as to why we were coming and what we were going to do. We talked with her mum beforehand and prepared in detail the most appropriate room in the house, who should be in the room and the time frame. This was imperative, as if we had not taken the time and thought about the impact on Milly we would not have been successful in gathering the information the ADOS should give us.

With Esther, it was the school observations which gave us the clues to why she was getting very angry at school. Without these observations, it would have been hard to convince school that she wasn't the 'stubborn, angry' girl they had described as she often didn't speak either.

When observing Esther at school, it became apparent that she relied heavily on transitional objects, familiar motivators that she needed around her to reduce anxiety and give some familiarity to her environment. However, these were little figurines. These were being interpreted by the teaching staff as a little girl just being stubborn about wanting to bring her toys into school. When you asked Esther, she could not tell you why she wanted them with her, just that she was having them with her. If anyone tried to take them off her, she was distressed. So this just reinforced the misunderstanding.

Esther had significant sensory sensitivities. Transitions were difficult. Being around people was difficult in the environment which she was in. When she did try to interact with her peers, she often found it confusing and overwhelming when the other children didn't want to talk about the things she was interested in. Esther was always better with an adult one to one. She could often communicate better with them, and they didn't judge her and accepted her silences and interests.

Once observed alongside her peers she became quite obvious in her characteristics and the evidence gathered from this part of the assessment heavily influenced the assessment process. This information also informed how I worked with her in sessions, as I then understood the need for transitional objects and their importance in my engagement with Esther and the ability to read when Esther was not able to engage or continue to engage. This informed my clinical practice, which in turn contributed to our successful therapeutic relationship.

When doing any assessment, it is important to be able to get the best from your young person, so consider having someone with them in the room whilst they are having their assessment. It's very rare we cannot be flexible enough in our practice or in the boundaries of assessments not to offer this.

Be thoughtful about how your young person understands you, particularly when they are experiencing high levels of anxiety. Uninformed clinicians may look at potentially 'more able' individuals as not fulfilling the criteria for a diagnosis. Areas of the assessments and questionnaires which may be missed are the areas around reciprocity and the use of gesturing. We see more and more that on the surface these key difficulties are masked by 'good enough' strategies the young women have learned. This is positive in terms of functioning but in terms of understanding themselves and others understanding them it is a huge disadvantage.

It is becoming evidenced through better recognition of ASC in girls and young women within mental health services that they often present with mental health difficulties prior to any other difficulties being spotted as the:

> 'pretence' they have to keep up in terms of mimicking and masking becomes physically and mentally draining consequently taking its toll on their emotional wellbeing. (Yaull-Smith 2008)

I think it important to mention *risk* at this point.

Within this client group risk is hard to measure and plan for, as acts of self-harm or attempts at taking their lives are often impulsive and reactive to an overwhelming/intense emotion or group of emotions or response to an inability to express and/ or understand what they are feeling and how to manage it at any one time. The most important thing is to stay vigilant and to try to ensure communication and monitoring remain open.

CHAPTER 8

Interventions and Strategies

Interventions and strategies are elements which are often not consistently provided within the package of care, because, unless you have skilled clinicians delivering these, then they are either delivered in a way which is not accessible to the individual, or they are not offered at all.

For me these are some fundamentals that are vital to obtaining any chance of engagement and meaningful work with our young women.

A key to any work with a young person is to use *their* words, *their* language, as this reduces anxiety and shows that you are trying to understand them and respect them. We so often use textbook words like anxiety and worry, yet these may not mean anything to our young people. Explore their words, ask permission to use them, check what they mean for that individual. Acknowledge and identify with the words they use. Mirror their use of words and normalise them. If they can't find the words, then use a different medium, such as colours, drawings and so on.

Before you start any intervention, ensure you have a clear indication of their cognitive profile. This will inform how to pitch your interventions, which medium works best for them and often to ascertain whether they have any processing difficulties. We all know this sounds idealistic, and for many of us it is, but use what you have and seek guidance from your educational and clinical psychologists.

Remember to modulate your praise of them, particularly if this is something your young woman struggles with. This is very important and often influences your therapeutic relationship. If you get this wrong, you can lose them. Find a way to praise in a way they can accept and process and explain why this is an important element of your work and future acceptance of self. This often feels alien to clinicians and quite clinical, but I can't stress enough how important it is. For parents and professionals there is a lot of stress on the importance of praise and the positive impact this has. We do it in particular ways in our lives and work, therefore we think that our young women should know how to expect and receive it. Praise and accepting it is a very personal thing and deserves respect and careful considerate management.

Think about time frames. Clinic times don't have to be an hour. They can be much shorter. Quality and appropriateness, not quantity, are key. Where we deliver our interventions is fundamental, and how we teach our strategies to be generalised and implemented is vital. For example, teaching about emotions from pictures in a clinic room after school is never going to be the best time or way to deliver this kind of work. We need to bear in mind the complexity of our young people and what they have had to negotiate during the day at school or at home, struggling with significant anxiety. Therefore expecting them to engage, process and then go away and implement and generalise, when we have probably already identified some difficulties within their executive functioning does not make sense. So, within your clinical and service limitations and belief systems, think about the most effective way to reach your young woman, as this will be your answer to your managers and commissioners when they question if your practices and services are cost effective.

Be mindful to maintain boundaries and compromise from the onset. Setting up contracts together with the young women which address mutual needs may enable positive shifts in moving toward the goal of addressing their emotional understanding and regulation. This works *with* the rigidity of thought and tackles their often strong sense of injustice; rather than pushing against their beliefs and inflexibilities work with and include them. Long gone are the days where we had one strategy fits all. The fundamental strategies which often work within the autistic spectrum still apply, but their implementation needs to be individualised.

I encountered a very recent example of this in a session with one of my clients. I was trying to ascertain good and bad emotions in the context of weeks of working with her around her emotional understanding and regulation and management. I was trying to explain the arousal cycle. The client was unable to understand my drawing and explanation, and I was losing her in the session. I stopped and checked that my observation was correct, and that in fact she was not understanding what I was talking about. I then asked a simple question: 'How would you draw when your mood changes? It can be from good to bad, or vice versa. Just show me how you would explain it me.' She drew a straight line which went from 'acid' to 'alkaline'. This resulted in a full-scale explanation of scientific numbers and ratios of what happens as she is getting worried, when this then moves into frustration, then anger and how that deescalated into worry and then sadness, and ultimately, after a time, into reflection on the situation. No emotive words were used, but the description allowed me to understand her emotions through her description using things she could align herself with.

When tackling emotional understanding and management in oneself and others remember we are all individuals and think in unique ways. The more I work with young women with ASC, the more they astonish me with their creative ways of understanding, expressing and communicating their emotions: ways we never explore or think about. Be creative too. Use their strengths and then build on those. Not everyone thinks happy is represented by orange or sadness with black. Not everyone can connect with the physiological sensations which alert them to shifts in feelings and emotions. Not everyone thinks that feelings and emotions are the same things. But we all feel and we all react and behave. It's our job to find the way in.

Use different modes and media when trying to engage in work with your young people. Acknowledge when you are not succeeding in getting your information across. You have to change direction, but only do so when you have ascertained their understanding and style of learning. Sometimes you can get so embroiled in a way of working that you can lose sessions. Some clinicians would finish here and not restart or change their stance or style. I'm not saying you will always find the answer/route/way but at least be flexible enough to try. As long as you can evidence your practice, you can justify the extra time that may be needed to ensure you find the right way/technique/intervention for your young person.

Take time to play to the young women's strengths, be honest, negotiate, test things out, use motivators, empathise, boundary and model.

Cognitive behaviour therapy, solution focused brief therapy, dialectic behaviour therapy and other talking therapies for these young women will need to be adapted to fit the individual, as they are experiencing different ways of thinking which were not often taken into consideration when these therapies were first introduced. Due to social communication difficulties and/or possible sensory processing and integration difficulties and potential restrictions with flexibility of thought, focus and concentration, planning and predicting, the original formats or ways these therapies were to be delivered may not be successful or helpful. This is where you will need to review and rethink whether you can adapt the therapy or style of delivery or whether you need to shift to a different form of therapy or way of working.

We need to be mindful of our expectations of our individual's speed and ability to change and learn, as fundamentally we are asking them to do something which is innately extremely difficult for them and, in some cases, impossible.

We need to clinically challenge ourselves and personally challenge our own belief systems of how things need to be done. Thus we need to ensure we receive and participate in regular professional development. It is important for us to stretch the boundaries of our therapies and to work on understanding our young women and adapt our practice and our own rigidity of thought accordingly.

> *Ruth*: Having appointments in school time was unsettling as she had lots of other appointments, and being at school became harder. She didn't like talking directly and would have preferred to be able to doodle and having the right person being able to understand her doodles. This is what now happens in high school. Doodling allows her to shorten answers, responding to questions.

Ruth: Talking... Life would be great if she didn't have to talk to anybody.

Ruth: She liked you because you talked about your dogs. You had good ideas, and she says you were less boring than all the other doctors she had to see.

Find a common ground. Find a way. It's always there, we just have to find it. Building that relationship takes time and clinical resilience, but don't forget there is something to be said for having some fun at times.

Here is a list of the interventions I tried with Milly. It was trial and error, perseverance on both sides and support from family which enabled the process.

MILLY

As part of my getting to understand Milly's life I asked Lisa to keep a diary of 'incidents', so we could look at antecedents/triggers, environment and so on, and then reflect on what could be done differently for and with Milly in the future. Here are some of Lisa's anecdotes:

Lisa: At times, I felt like I was being treated like her personal slave, Milly was becoming more and more defiant. I truly believe Milly has no concept of how she makes others feel, and even when this is explained in detail, she appears to have no apparent understanding, and more disappointingly than that, no desire to make it right again. I don't want to shy away from my responsibilities as a parent, but I want harmony at home, and I can't tread on eggshells for the rest of my life.

Giving me examples of difficult situations gave me insight into some of the executive functioning difficulties Milly may have been experiencing and enabled me to think of ways of supporting Milly to hopefully ensure she could overcome or learn to manage her difficulties.

Here are some of the areas in which Milly was experiencing difficulties:

- using the telephone, will answer if no one else in the house (but not always) but will never make a call to perhaps ask information about, for example, opening times, to reserve an item or any other enquiry

- out and about, asking for directions

- on a bus, saying the destination, asking for the fare

- ordering in a café, will forgo food and drink if cannot see something she likes rather than ask for something else to be served

- paying for items, asking how much, rather than just handing over notes, and applying social niceties

- situations which involve choice/decision making

- showing an interest in others

- affording other people the right to an opinion

- having an appreciation that she is not always right

- understanding life is not black and white

- anxious over timekeeping

- managing shutdowns

- aloof

- social isolation

- fight

- flight

- control

- lack of empathy

- planning and organisation difficulties

- relationship difficulties

- limited understanding of impact of behaviour on others
- significant difficulty understanding her own affect and how that impacts on others
- no social filter in terms of bluntness and saying it how it is
- food restriction
- obsessions
- excessive personal hygiene
- revision
- avoidance.

Reflections on scenarios of behavioural difficulties

These were often done with Lisa, as Milly at that time often found it difficult to talk with me. When Milly was able to engage, she could often participate, as she had had processing time and was calm enough to at least listen to what had happened and how situations could be addressed and managed differently from all aspects and from the perspectives of all of those involved. These were often difficult conversations and uncomfortable for all involved, as there was a fine balance between being helpful and productive and what could be interpreted as negative, but it gave some framework for discussion and moving forward. An example of this:

> *Lisa*: I am becoming increasingly concerned at Milly's continued lashing out with her hand, slapping anyone who makes a remark she would rather they didn't.

Modelling around social communication and social interaction

We can laugh about this now, and have since we have met up again. At the time this became my way of letting Milly know how the impact of her style of communication impacted on me. I described when in interactions with Milly how her tone and manner made me feel and how this could change my interactions and relationship with her.

Sensory assessment

This was very important for Milly, for the building of knowledge for Milly about herself, as Milly was not for accepting much at this point (sorry Milly, but it's the truth), but also for Lisa, Andy and Izzy who had borne the brunt (Milly will not mind me saying this) of her sensitivities for years, especially Andy with her aversion to his deodorant and aftershave. Even though the strategies we were taught to give at the time by experienced clinicians, experts in their fields, often matched the sensory issue, they often didn't complement the individual's need and their personality or social needs, for example, offering a strategy of ear defenders to be worn in public to combat oversensitivity to sound in crowded places, when the individual's overriding need is to fit in and not look different.

That being said, there are many more gadgets on the market now which can do the job we need them to do whilst not drawing attention to the individuals who want to merge in and not look different. I am also a more confident clinician around sensory items these days so can be much more flexible in my recommendations of alternatives which equate to the original advice.

Family work

This was crucial, and Milly's family couldn't have been more engaged or more motivated to understand Milly and themselves. Due to the nature of Milly's journey through services, and therefore Lisa and Andy's, it was imperative that I do the family work. This wasn't me doing something out of my clinical expertise or role, merely an extension of my skills with supervision from clinicians expert in this field. To be completely honest it was working in an integrative way with the family, not delivering family therapy. Sometimes the individual and their family need to be given the opportunity to continue with the person they have forged that therapeutic relationship with. This can be helpful to both sides and in a well-functioning team, by that I mean with sound clinical supervision in place, with the appropriate skill mix and expertise this should be encouraged. Lisa, Andy and Izzy were my eyes and ears. They helped me understand the dynamics, the stresses and strains, their side of the story. Without them my knowledge and understanding of Milly would have been limited. Through their involvement

Milly did begin to engage and trust me and would participate in the group sessions and in conversations and reflections.

Liaison with school

This was an intense and intensive piece of work which involved education of girls on the spectrum. This was seven years ago. We knew even less then, so it won't come as a surprise that the school had never experienced a young woman like Milly and for a considerable amount of time had great difficulty understanding why Milly was involved in services. At school, certainly in the early years of secondary school, Milly was a model pupil, intelligent, quiet and studious. When they heard Lisa and Andy describing what happened at home and the impact of the stress of school and the social impact, they were stunned and for a while disbelieving. Lisa and Andy had to endure many meetings where we battled. It was a battle for them to even consider our recommendation for an assessment of ASC. Milly also was not keen for us to speak with her teachers, so it was a very uncomfortable time all round. Professionally it was extremely frustrating and isolating. I found myself in a setting where many teachers had input into the various conversations, some vehemently disagreeing with my clinical formulation. Balancing this with distressed and frustrated parents battling a system that did not believe them was clinically extremely challenging.

As the school years passed, it was the social element, the planning and organisation of the day and the homework and revision, which were impacting on Milly's wellbeing. The gap between Milly and her peers in terms of socialising and planning aspects became more and more evident. School finally got on board. In the end they were supportive and did manage to get specialists to enable Milly to manage things like revision in a more helpful way.

Perseverance is the key. When you know, and you have your evidence, don't give up. You are that young woman's key person. You are responsible and accountable for their emotional wellbeing. You are their ambassador and the family's support line. Often families like the families of the girls in this book do not reach criteria for social care, nor do they often need it. So you are often the person who knows the most about your young person, sometimes even more than extended family. Your knowledge and perspective are critical in the wider understanding for the young women you work with.

Visual aids to help with organisation and planning

Milly eventually got help from the educational team who specialise in ASC in terms of her learning styles, but we also worked on timetables for revision and mind mapping types of ideas and examples.

Monitoring of mood

This was difficult initially, as Milly had significant difficulty matching her physiological feelings with her emotional state, so warning signs of deterioration in mood or any fluctuation in emotional regulation were almost non-existent. This does not mean that the feelings weren't there. They were there in intensity and frequency but not recognisable or linked enough for Milly to recognise and manage. Sometimes they were overwhelming and all consuming, and suddenly Milly would go into shutdown for days. This would impact on all her physical and emotional states. Her parents would be rendered helpless to assist Milly, not only because often they didn't get much warning but also due to Milly's inability to express how she was feeling so she became uncommunicative and self-isolating.

So we all moved from what appeared to be low mood to catastrophic shutdown suddenly and for long periods of time. At the time, this was terrifying for me as a clinician and emotionally exhausting and frightening for Milly and her parents. Support to Lisa and Andy was crucial at these times, and often Lisa would come to appointments to talk and off load and re-energise before going back home.

What we learned over time, and know now, is that Milly needs time to shut down and recharge. She has described this in this book. Now she has learnt to regulate and manage her life, so she doesn't crash and burn so often. She modulates her week, her life, in order to stabilise her emotional thermometer. She has learnt to self-regulate.

Working on emotional understanding and management

This was very difficult for Milly, and to continue work of this nature with someone who is finding it so difficult whilst being intelligent enough to know she should be able to understand is difficult. We did some family sessions involving Lisa, Andy and Izzy so as to take the focus off Milly. But more in-depth work proved unhelpful to Milly. Milly knew how she was feeling. It was just that understanding the complexities and their context and management was difficult for her to negotiate.

Sometimes individuals and their families need time to process and implement before embarking on further clinical interventions, but that should be assessed and reviewed in the individual's best interests and with sound clinical evidence, not because clinicians don't ask for supervision and clinical support and guidance, not because waiting times are more important than lives, not because the first therapy offered isn't helpful or accessible for them.

DARCEY

Darcey was different. Darcey was eager to understand and be understood. At the time I was working with Darcey it was more heavily weighted to Darcey wanting to be understood. Darcey was frustrated and confused as to why people didn't understand why she thought and behaved like she did. If they modified their behaviour things would be more manageable. She was and remains driven, ambitious, intelligent, fearless, but also sensitive and anxious.

Reflection

From the outset Darcey found it helpful to look at times that caused her distress and look at what had happened and why she had reacted as she had. That being said, initially this was to justify Darcey's behaviour, which at the time manifested itself with extremes of distress, anxiety, frustration and anger. Darcey's intention at no point was to absolve herself of all responsibility for her actions. She merely wanted to know why things escalated, why she felt so overwhelmed with emotion which she found hard to regulate.

ASC information sharing

Once Darcey received her diagnosis, she was eager to understand what that meant for her, how her thinking differently would impact on her and how she could manage, knowing she had many ambitions in life. Darcey compiled a PowerPoint presentation which she did indeed present to me. This was so important for her and marked a huge milestone in her recognition of herself and the beginning of her acceptance of her diagnosis. For me this was a moment of recognition that sometimes your clinical expertise pays off and someone has benefited from it. Darcey shared her diagnosis with her closest friends at school. Her family and extended family have always been aware and supported her and loved her for her first and foremost. She embraced her school being made aware and is proud that now the school she attended is more aware, supportive and helpful to all different kinds of additional needs. When she was first diagnosed, she was in the minority, if not the only one with a diagnosis of an additional need.

Externalisation

This was something very new to me and not something a learning disability nurse would ever have known about or used, so I am grateful to Michaela, the clinician who taught me to deliver this. This has become something I use now as a matter of course, because it takes away the emotion from the individual and allows the resilient features of that individual to manage a difficult emotion with their skills. I have found it helpful, particularly with younger children and with those who have difficulty connecting emotionally, as an initial step to understanding and managing emotions in a positive helpful way. Darcey took to this so well and her externalisation of anger became 'Verruca'.

Role modelling

Darcey worked better either alone or with one of her parents present. This wasn't true role modelling, more me acting out similarly to an episode described by Darcey's parents. I would get Darcey to comment on the behaviour and start to understand what the impact on her and others could be if she behaved in this way.

Family work

Family work had too many dimensions for Darcey. Needless to say, the family were heavily involved but in a different way to Milly. Kelly and Ashley would meet with me separately at times, and they would take it in turns to join Darcey in her sessions. Her sister was regularly present but not always in the sessions, as these were seen as Darcey's sessions to learn.

> *Kelly*: CAMHS also took time out to support her sister Freya who often suffered at the end of Darcey's behaviours and time with the school, introducing the ideas of supporting these kinds of special needs.

Behavioural work

Lots of reflective scenarios were discussed and analysed with Kelly and Ashley in order to try and establish functions and triggers for the anger and anxiety. This was a relaxed form of behavioural functional analysis in order for us to further understand why Darcey communicated through behaviour and why she presented with emotional dysregulation. A full functional analysis would have been too intrusive for this family. This is where using your skills differently and with more clinical flexibility comes into play. This gave us vital information in relation to Darcey's difficulties with executive functioning, understanding social contexts, inflexibility of thought, significant sensory sensitivities and word and particular sentence structure processing difficulties. Behavioural interventions were not the way forward for Darcey; understanding the functions of the behaviour, educating Darcey and her parents in the functions and then finding strategies to support Darcey were the way forward.

Acknowledging and understanding sensory processing difficulties and managing sensory sensitivities

Darcey had difficulties with mealtimes, with food, the expectations of the social etiquette of eating, the planning before the eating, and finishing what she was doing in order to eat. Another issue was her dad playing music in his study in the evening. The bass in the music he listened to was the most difficult for Darcey to tolerate. It wasn't the sound, more the depth and breadth of the beat and the vibration. These may sound like the usual gripes we have in families, and they were, but the difference was the impact these elements had on Darcey's emotional regulation and therefore the impact on the family as a whole.

Darcey's other sensory processing difficulty, which was impacting on her learning, was colours. Once we had worked out which colours of pens on which coloured backgrounds were easier for her to read and implemented overlays into school and for her homework, this reduced one element of frustration and confusion in her day.

ESTHER

Esther was a strong-willed and determined individual with a beautiful sensitivity and vulnerability about her. She liked to people watch, and was always strikingly honest with a wonderfully kind side to her. Interventions with Esther were built over time through her mum Ruth in order to address her emotional dysregulation, particularly when at school.

Liaison with school and observations within school

This was the main area of work, as this was the place Esther was having difficulty with and vice versa. The impact on her emotional wellbeing was escalating and having detrimental effects on her learning and accessing her lessons. The observations gave me insight into both parties' problems, which then helped me in my work with Ruth. I could explain to Ruth what I had seen on my visits into school and became the middle woman when it came to communication with the school. The outcomes of my observations needed to educate and support the school as much as Esther in order for Esther to benefit. Ruth and Esther needed to know that I had seen what they had been explaining to me in terms of the distress and behaviour, but it was extremely important to work with the school and listen to their perspective to ensure appropriate behaviour, practical and sensory interventions were implemented, and they understood the importance of my advice.

When you work in different services to your own, be mindful of their understanding, the language they use and the guidance they have to adhere to, as you will find that you are coming from different perspectives, experiences and with differing expectations. You and the staff need to find common ground so you can achieve the best service for your young client.

Between the school, Ruth (Esther's mum), the education department's specialist services for ASC and I implemented and used some of the existing practical strategies Esther had already been using. There needed to be negotiation, as the strategies Esther was using were against school behaviour management policy but with the school's new understanding and seeing Esther's response to being allowed to use her strategies they agreed. Esther used transitional objects. She would carry particular objects (which were usually linked with an existing obsession/special interest) with her which would help her move around her environment. She liked to have her things of special interest around her so she was allowed some on her desk and some in her drawers. She had scheduled timetabled time to spend with these objects. This meant that she knew that they were a constant and a reward in her day.

Her positioning in class was crucial. She needed to have her own desk, but she also wanted access to other children she liked, so she was encouraged and did at times participate in group work when it was engineered thoughtfully by the teacher. Not making her conform but including her was a real winner. Esther knew the rules, but sometimes her sensory issues and emotional dysregulation did not allow her to access these times, but when she was regulated and motivated she could. Allowing her time to process was so important.

Externalisation and relaxation techniques

The same principles applied when I saw Esther in clinic. She had her transitional objects, and they were always made welcome. If Esther was having difficulty with the spoken word, Ruth and I would talk about things, and sometimes we would wait, and sometimes we would do something else which was more fun as Esther has a wicked sense of humour. These sessions were sometimes the best, as I got to see Esther relaxed and able to laugh at herself and others. I could witness her skills and resilience and her ability to communicate effectively.

Esther did engage with externalisation and did use the skills she had learned from time to time.

> *Ruth*: We were offered ongoing support and parenting courses which we accepted and started working with Fiona. I would love to say I remember all the sessions and what we did, but my brain isn't that good. I do remember that they were based around what Esther wanted help with. Understanding her emotions was an important part, what they were and being able to recognise them. Drawing Esther on flip-chart paper, clenched fists, getting hot were two of the identifiable reactions she had to getting angry or stressed. Ways to de-stress included 'pigs in the mud', which we changed to her brothers in the mud and blowing out the stress. Stubborn Ben, her externalisation character (previously discovered and created by another colleague with Esther) was discussed a few times, and I think made an appearance every so often. Esther also had a colour thing which she took to school, blue calm, green happy, red angry. She could show the colour on her desk, so her teacher knew how she was feeling. Fiona also helped in school observing a lesson and making suggestions. Liaising when the school brought in a specialist teaching service to do exactly what Fiona was already working on. For me the most important part of this was being supported. Giving me the tools and the confidence to support Esther. Focusing on what she was good at, the positives and thinking of strategies to support her through what she wasn't. Also having the confidence when dealing with the head teacher of the school's refusal to provide Esther any TA (teaching assistant) support and also putting strategies in place with her class teachers.

THINGS TO LOOK OUT FOR IN WORK WITH A CLIENT

Dig deep into emotional understanding

Don't just ask if they can label emotions, as this can be catastrophically misleading. Check and recheck. Ask what they understand. Ask for examples. Ask for their explanations and their words.

And when you think you have checked, check again and check in different environments to see if they can generalise. Ask what you would see in them when exhibiting a certain emotion and what they would see in others.

Watch body language and eye contact

Signs of panic and anxiety can be missed. Watch for rapid breathing, self-strangulation for deep pressure. This sounds quite dramatic and can be misconstrued, but I have had numerous experiences of my young people looking like they are strangling themselves in session when what they are doing is applying deep pressure to manage the anxiety and their vocalisations. Picking is quite common, but if you spot it, it can give you clues as to how to shift your session or gauge the emotional state of your young person. Don't just dismiss it as a sensory thing or a fidget. Try to find the function, so you can work with it, not against it.

Look out for signs of hyperactivity

Check out the hyperactivity (often misunderstood for ADHD). In what contexts does it show itself and how? In young women hyperactivity is frequently driven by anxiety and not knowing how to express and manage their energy. Don't rule out ADHD, but check it with the paediatricians.

Notice variations in eye contact

When is it better? Is it better when interested in or motivated about what you are talking about or what you are doing? Use this knowledge to weave into building the resilience of interactions. Shift and move the content of your interaction. When you have an established positive relationship, you can tackle the cause of the unusual modulation of eye contact and can incorporate when you notice it going and returning, how it impacts on you and the conversation or activity you are engaged in. Acknowledge it's OK to lose eye contact whilst ensuring you communicate the positive impact their eye contact has on you emotionally.

Reciprocity

This is the one that always makes me chuckle: not about the young person but the clinicians. Reciprocity with girls is harder to spot, as they often learn enough to make you think they are interested. But if you challenge that interest, the response you will invariably get is that they know they need to appear interested but really are not interested at all. Their conversation can be very deceptive. If you catch them on something they are interested in it will appear and feel reciprocal. This is a major item as during the ADOS girls/young women often don't score as they can do enough to appear to have a four-element conversation, building on your comments.

Do they know anything about their friends,
their interests, their families?
Are they bothered? If the young women's relationships are connected to mutual interests, then they are more likely to tell you that they do know about their friends. If you dig deeper, it will often be that they know joint interest information and basics about their friend's situations, but will rarely go into deeper conversation or more 'off piste' conversational topics about relationships or emotions or interests outside their common interests. This is not always because they can't be bothered, but sometimes because when they have experienced conversations going in this way they often find them challenging and awkward. Watch out for scripted reciprocity. Check it out. Question deeper.

Executive function

How often do we come across our young women having difficulties planning, organising themselves, tidying up, predicting what might happen in the future or navigating their way around a conversation? Are these issues with executive function, or is it part of difficulties with social imagination or attention and focus?

SUGGESTED STRATEGIES

There are many strategies that can be used with our young people, but don't think you can only use these, or that these are the only interventions to work. Mix and match. Try them but don't rely on them. Here are some examples:

Comic strip

These are often very useful when reflecting on situations and if your young person has difficulty expressing themselves through speech.

Visuals

These include timetables, schedules, emotion cards and your externalisation characters. These can help with executive functioning and with organising the day or particular tasks. Remember to match the intervention to the individual though; be flexible and use what motivates or interests them.

Remember when using them to check whether vertical or horizontal works best and what colours in terms of pens and background colours.

Spider diagrams

These are helpful when trying to put thoughts down on paper and organise thoughts. They could be beneficial when revising.

Sensory assessments

These are often hard to obtain but invaluable. Check with your paediatrician, CAMHS and your education service. If no one does them in your area then there are private practitioners who will assess and advise on practical interventions.

Diaries

For our budding writers and poets, this is often a good way for our young people to document difficulties and how they managed or didn't manage. It often gives us as clinicians insight into their emotional understanding and can be very helpful if they are experiencing times of distress or relationship difficulties.

Motivators

These are crucial to our individuals. Motivators need to be incorporated into any behavioural shifts you are wanting to work on with your young people as well as respecting their influence and impact on the individual. Motivators must never be taken away but can be used within a contract with your young person or within reward systems.

Ensure routines are still accessible in times of change

This can be possible at times of unexpected change if discussed and practised previously at times when things were stable.

OTHER AREAS OF SIGNIFICANT IMPORTANCE YOU MUST INCLUDE IN YOUR CLINICAL PRACTICE

Parenting

Always engage parents/carers. There are many ways of doing this and there needs to be careful consideration as families are complex and different. Sometimes there needs to be work with the family members separately, sometimes in conjunction with the young person, but make sure you assess the right path for your family. If the girls/young women are in care include carers and social workers.

School

Do not work in isolation. Liaise and work collaboratively with the relevant people in your young person's school. Schools are often the most challenging of places for them and they need us to make sure we communicate what we are doing and what we know with people who are important to them within their educational setting.

Acknowledgment and eventual celebration of differences

This is where you want to get to, as this means acceptance and embracing of being different, as Temple Grandin would say, 'different but not less' (Grandin and Attwood 2012). This will bring with it understanding of self, which leads onto increased confidence and self-esteem and the beginnings of understanding others.

Challenge

Don't be afraid to challenge your young people, your families and other services. If individuals or services do not implement your advice or your strategies ensure you involve them in your reviews, check out why and see how you can help them. Don't push against them, work collaboratively; it is after all in the best interests of the individual.

Boundary

Consider this not only in terms of your sessions but your interactions as well. There is a difference between being humane and sharing appropriate relevant personal information with your young people and crossing professional boundaries. We expect and almost demand our young people and their families to share their most personal feelings, and we see them at their most raw and vulnerable, so some compassion and care is needed. Otherwise you won't capture that special relationship you need to enable your young people to grow and manage.

Be clear

Keep a check on your language. It's so easy to talk and not check if you are being understood. Avoid using flowery language and complex sentences. Remember you are working with young people who have difficulties with their social communication.

Be flexible

Adapt your practice to their needs. Go for walks. Build a den. Go to their home. Do what is best for them. If you initially 'go to them', they will 'come to you'.

Monitor and review your interventions and strategies

This should be done regularly, whilst giving them enough time to be implemented.

Watch out for them telling you what they want you to hear

This is so common. If you are doubtful, investigate further.

Remember to include generalising and practice

Doing work in sessions will not be naturally generalised, so this is when family and school and so on are important in ensuring what has been learned is embedded into everyday life.

Watch for anxiety and loss of attention, restlessness, stimming, conduct behaviours

Check your environment, check whether they need time out, break the sessions up. You may need to have some physical activity merged into your sessions or some breathing and mindfulness.

With any interaction with your young person be mindful that they may get overwhelmed

This happens particularly with attention to detail in their surroundings and may impact on their focus and concentration.

Be aware of distractions

This is always difficult when you see young people in their school – there are alarms, bells, lots of moving around. Try to find places with minimal changes or distractions.

Respect their 'comfort zone'

If your young person needs to keep their hood up or sit facing the wall or sit under a table with no shoes on then so be it. Expecting them to sit in a clinical setting to discuss things they find considerably anxiety provoking without having any of their 'comfort zone' available is bordering on cruel.

Be aware of the need to filter

If your young person is losing concentration, consider that they may be having difficulty trying to prioritise the noises they are aware of and filter unimportant noises out. It is important to get them to reference you from time to time, as they may not have the ability or be too overwhelmed to know when to listen to you.

Watch out for overload

This can lead to a meltdown and ultimately to a shutdown. Milly talks about this and needing to isolate herself in order to rejuvenate.

Be mindful of difficulties separating reality from fantasy

Safety can be a major issue, as young women find difficulty learning consequences of actions and may not learn from experience.

Risk

Girls and young women can sometimes have difficulty imagining risk so they go ahead anyway.

Notice repetitive thought, not just actions

This can be repetitively wanting to get things right and becoming a perfectionist to the point of detriment.

Be mindful of using words with multiple meanings

Be careful around words in general, not only in their multiple meanings but also don't presume that we are using the same meanings for the same words. Always explore this and find their words.

MEDICATION

In addition to being a learning disability nurse I am also a non-medical prescriber (nurse prescriber). There are many benefits which come from having these additional specialist skills and knowledge. This combination is rare but extremely valuable to young women who may need to explore medication at points in their life and may need that specialist combination to aid their recovery and/or stabilisation.

The model of non-medical prescribers fits into service development and service enrichment. The value of using clinicians with additional skills intensifies the therapeutic relationship for the individual as they know that you not only have a relationship with them but with their behaviour and clinical presentation, enabling you to monitor their mood with more informed information and knowledge as you have previous experience of them to measure against. It also benefits them and the consultant as information sharing to the consultant gives up-to-date accurate reporting and translation of their current emotional wellbeing to the doctor responsible for their care.

I decided to qualify as a non-medical prescriber to understand what medications the young people I was working with were prescribed, so I could monitor them whilst on medication to inform clinical decisions. Knowing how medications work, their side effects and contraindications is important when you are monitoring, observing and assessing behaviour as they can not only improve and stabilise mood, which in turn impacts on behaviour, but can exaggerate and exacerbate sensory difficulties, increase anxiety, or stabilise one condition but in turn enhance features of comorbidities. It also gives a clearer, fuller picture for the overseeing consultant psychiatrist. As the practitioner who sees the young person regularly and in all contexts and settings you can notice and document shifts in behaviour, which is imperative when dosages and types of medications need to be considered.

I embarked on the course as it was evident that there was an increase in demand and need to offer medication to those individuals with ASC who experience high levels of anxiety, obsessions and low mood. This, however, is in conjunction with psychological therapies, in order to promote and maintain a good mental health status. Sometimes anxiety has such a vice-like grip on our young people's minds that they cannot access therapy and just need a virtual crutch, while they can commence with their understanding of themselves and what is happening to them.

Milly has experienced the benefits of medication:

Milly: I started Propranolol (from GP) in about Jan/Feb 2012 after my first exams at college, as I had started having my first panic attacks. I took them as and when I needed them, e.g. before exams or other events. I started Sertraline in the summer of 2014. Since the January of 2014 I had started to become increasingly anxious to the point in about March where I wasn't sleeping or eating, and I was struggling to leave my flat to attend lectures. I had gone to the university doctor, where I had been told to take Propranolol three times a day, and then when I came home for the summer, I went to the GP, who prescribed Sertraline (50mg a day). I was very anxious about actually taking it, because I was worried about side effects, but once I had been on it for a couple of weeks it made a massive difference, and I have been on it ever since.

Milly's medication is reviewed regularly and enables her to lead a less anxious life. Milly approaches the taking of medication responsibly and in conjunction with the other elements we need to ensure a healthy mind. She climbs (how impressive is that?), goes to the gym, sees her family and friends when she needs to, rations her social interaction so it is enough but she also gets the space she so definitely needs and identifies in herself to recharge.

Neither Darcey nor Esther currently or previously take any medication in relation to emotional wellbeing.

Medication, like labels, splits the autism community and clinicians and therefore there needs to be training and a greater understanding of the role of medication. My belief and clinical opinion is that if the young people I am working with are so crippled with anxiety or low mood and unable to access life let alone therapy, then in conjunction with a therapy which is tailored to their needs, an encouragement to exercise in a way they find helpful, a diet which fuels them sufficiently and without too much challenge on their sensory or rigid ways of coping and some relaxation which they benefit from, I feel it should be considered.

I often feel that anxiety is misunderstood and misconstrued in this particular group of young people as it can manifest itself in different guises; also it is not prevalent in all settings. I am sometimes concerned, too, about what we expect our young people to tolerate before we assess medication for them; sometimes they become more unwell and more emotionally dysregulated whilst they try to survive.

Something being used much more in clinic settings is pet therapy. However, if you do not have such a forward-thinking/thinking-out-of-the-box kind of provision in your service, sometimes doing home visits or going on dog walks with the young people's dogs or sitting with them can aid conversations to flow better and can reduce anxiety, as well as enable your communication and interaction with your young person to be more relaxing, thus more productive and more helpful.

EXERCISE

Hans Asperger, the Austrian doctor who defined Asperger syndrome in 1944, described advising exercise in the daily interventions. This has been used in various guises over the years, but this emphasis has become diluted. My clinical experience evidences that, in order to enhance concentration and general emotional wellbeing, exercise is fundamental as it produces and maintains healthy and productive minds. Darcey danced from an early age and taught herself yoga. She skis, swims and engages regularly in physical activity. Milly found climbing at age ten and continues to climb.

Enabling them to balance their own emotional and physical energy is important and something we need to incorporate into our work with our young women, alongside them learning to communicate when they need to balance.

CHAPTER 9

Clinical and Service Culture Change

Mental health services for children and young people are in the midst of change. Change is definitely needed and welcomed by the clinicians and the children, young people and families. However, where does this client group sit within these changes and where does the expertise come from to support and embed change?

Currently the pathways for children and young people with ASC or undiagnosed social communication difficulties often fall between learning disability services and/or CAMHS services or in between services, resulting in no service provision. The way the pathways are set up and function varies within trusts, let alone counties. Who manages them also differs, so in some areas the pathways are joint and are termed neurodevelopmental pathways, which encompass other conditions such as ADHD. Some are run separately from paediatric services. Some are run from CAMHS services, and some are beginning to be jointly run between services.

There is also the independent sector, which diagnoses children and young people, but often if this is the route, parents opt for it for their children. If /when they try to access service in the National Health Service, the reports are often not accepted, which means that the young person has to go through another assessment process.

Eligibility criteria differ significantly. Although there is guidance on good practice, there is no policed standardised consistent pathway for assessment diagnosis and treatment. Currently waiting lists average 12–24 months from initial referral to assessment but, in some areas, this can be longer. Timely appropriate assessments are vital.

Assessments are also being diluted to cut corners and time to get through huge waiting lists, putting clinicians and standardised testing at risk, making clinicians vulnerable and minimising research-based assessments. So quantity often is addressed, but the quality of getting through the quantity is compromised.

Essential observations which need to be executed in the home and school are often cut from the assessment process as these take time and are not on 'the checklist'. What they give you, however, is qualitative data about natural events. You see children interacting in their natural environment, and you see the 'real person'. These settings provide essential information, as without these all you have are people's opinions on questionnaires and formal assessments. Surely our young people deserve quality assessments in order to inform clinical decision making? From my experience, without these and without clinicians present to represent their young people's clinical presentation, you have panels of clinicians working off checklists and limited information. This results in indecision, further assessments and delaying of diagnosis for some people, which can impact on their emotional wellbeing, which impacts on families and support networks which impacts on education… invest from the beginning and everyone wins.

Once diagnosis has been given what happens next is a lottery. The standard of support, interventions and strategies varies, as do the opinions of who is best to deliver those services and how and when they are delivered.

What is imperative and comes before resources and technology is tenacity, compassion, time and flexibility of thought and practice. You need to be knowledgeable, evidence based and up to date of course, but humanity in relationships is what you are entering into – the therapeutic relationship is imperative. Sometimes stress of workload, minimal staffing and service limitations take their toll on you as individuals and clinicians, but at the end of the day we are here to enable our young people to be emotionally resilient and to reach their full potential. This means we have a responsibility to model that, and the services we work for have a responsibility to ensure they support us so we can do just that. Working in a restrictive system with financial and clinical limitations can be frustrating, but you can always find a way to be the best at what you do. You must strive for that excellence, as it will be that excellence that will impact on an individual's life.

If we get the service, pathways, understanding and skill mix right, the impact on our young women's resilience and the sustainability of their emotional wellbeing will be significant. This encourages longevity and productivity in their lives and in their communities. In terms of positive outcomes and value for money it will enable efficient appropriate clinical throughput, ensuring a more qualititative and efficient pathway, which will reduce complaints and carouselling of individuals into services.

Most services hold clinics that are 9am–5pm, Monday to Friday, on the whole. Although there are moves afoot to change the way our services deliver care pathways to our clients, currently this is when we expect families to be able to see us. When you have identified that intensive work with families and individuals is needed, these rigidities impact on their work and schooling. This can be detrimental to their lives and can impact on their emotional wellbeing, for example, when parents are unable to make appointments due to work commitments or childcare difficulties. Services need to be thinking differently in terms of allowing clinicians time and flexibility of practice to be able to build a therapeutic relationship with their young person, and identifying at the point of referral who will be best equipped to work with that individual and their family. It seems we need to get across that there needs to be more emphasis on the therapeutic alliance and what that looks like and how individual clinicians can work more flexibly and creatively.

There has been extensive research and dialogue around therapeutic alliance, but you can't regurgitate it from a book; a relationship is complex and multi-faceted. If you match need with appropriate skill you are more likely to have a relationship formed early on which has more chance of a positive outcome for that person. In order to promote this, though, there must be a sound knowledge of the team from managers and clinical leads to not only appropriately allocate at the point of referral but to audit and track their service demand and fight for appropriate shifts in skill mixes and expertise.

Time for continuing professional development in the form of learning, research and conferences needs to be embedded in job plans, valued and encouraged and modelled by senior managers. A commitment is needed by managers to ensure clinicians keep up to date with their skills, so being encouraged and enabled to go on top-up days is imperative.

Family work needs to be promoted and encouraged within families. This can be done flexibly and thoughtfully as often flexibility and creativity are required from the practitioner to tailor practice to need.

There needs to be a national approach to standardised gold standard assessments and treatments, with trained staff to deliver the pathways from assessment, treatment and continued consultation to the family and the remaining support systems in place once that pathway has been completed. This builds on families and individual's resilience.

Regular planned and timetabled audits and reviews need to be carried out in order to ensure services are adapting to shifting trends in need.

Shadowing of staff in terms of management and clinical practice is imperative, as this not only keeps senior managers in touch with clinical situations but enables them to monitor clinical effectiveness and advise accordingly. In this type of work we often deliver care as lone workers. There are appropriate multi-disciplinary discussions, but observations of clinical input into sessions is often not monitored enough to ensure a standard of excellent service delivery is maintained.

Emelie Daniels is a Senior Nurse Practitioner (Mental Health Nurse) currently working within Tier 3 CAMHS. We have been working closely together with numerous young women who have been missed or misdiagnosed. During one of our reflections/clinical supervision sessions we discussed these young women. Emelie summarised how clinicians from mental health backgrounds approach referrals:

Emelie: A general approach to working with young people within mental health services upon receiving a referral – we read the referral, pulling out key observations and start to think of a therapeutic approach to support the young person. This is usually in reference to a psychological model as stated within the National Institute of Clinical Guidance. We gather further information and start to introduce themes or models which we believe have the best evidence and outcomes for that mental health condition. However, with young people with autistic traits, having this approach is presumptuous of their understanding of their emotional literacy. A young person may not know what anxiety looks or feels like; they may use an entirely different word. In these circumstances our approach needs to change. We need to go back, gain an understanding of all the emotions they access, what they feel like to them and how they express them before we can proceed with challenging the presenting mental health difficulty.

Joint working across grades and disciplines of staff needs to be encouraged to ensure quality. Practical elements need to be addressed, like ensuring the right equipment is available and tools which are needed for assessments and treatments are up to date and available. Physical environments need addressing and making more user friendly. Different types of therapies need investigating, which sometimes fit more with this particular client group than the narrow pathways we currently have available within a mental health setting. In relation to specifics, there need to be budgets available and reflective of need to access the most up-to-date diagnostic tools to enable the practitioner to be as contemporaneous as possible. Reflective practice should be integral in team/clinical meetings so you learn and adapt practice and identify service gaps.

It is important to emphasise that even now the age of discharge and eligibility still varies throughout the UK, resulting in an inconsistency of service provision and in some areas a complete service deficiency.

Lisa: Previously I had hated coming to CAMHS, the implication being that I was a failure as a parent. I felt judged and that my parenting skills were under scrutiny and, in all seriousness, that was just from the receptionists! Had I not needed the service so badly I would have put in a complaint against them. I don't imagine anyone chooses to go there, you are already probably at an all time low and that just adds to your misery.

In summary, our concerns should have been taken seriously earlier; there were many missed opportunities. There was an apparent lack of knowledge, understanding and interest of Asperger's in girls among the professionals we first encountered at CAMHS, despite Milly classically displaying all the behaviours from a very early age. Furthermore, there was no signposting to other support when she failed to respond to the 'mainstream' offerings of measuring her feelings on an emotional scale. Whilst we appreciate that Asperger's presents differently in girls we still, as a family, feel we could have been spared much anguish over the years and improved matters greatly for Milly by implementing strategies sooner had this been investigated on either of her previous referrals.

We need to regain the trust of this client group. Services have been disjointed, inconsistent and below par for this particular client group for a long time. The obvious answer is to use people who have been through the system to feed back. We need more participation: not a token gesture but true participation which leads to change. Here is some feedback from our families.

Milly: Having appointments out of school hours and at home [made a difference], I was ashamed enough about the situation as I already felt so different from my peers, so not having to leave class to go to appointments and also not needing to go to CAMHS itself was a big help. I would have appreciated the opportunity to meet other young women who had been diagnosed, so I didn't feel so alone and so we could have shared our thoughts about it. Most girls want to fit in and have friends and be 'normal', so working with them to improve communication skills and to learn to avoid (as much as possible) social faux pas. I think it is important to offer support for mental health issues. For girls, having been masking the problems for so long at school can really take its toll. I should have been involved with the process. As a reasonably intelligent young woman, I was mostly aware of what was happening but it is useful for someone to sit down and say, 'this is what's going on, you should expect this, this and this'. I didn't want a label, I wanted the whole thing to go away, but it felt like it was being forced upon me with no opportunity to discuss it. It would be helpful for some to explain why it might be useful to have this official label for the future. Continuing the support after the diagnosis was helpful.

Lisa and Andy: The referral process needs to be quicker. The post-diagnostic service needs to continue for much longer to provide ongoing support strategies to both the individual and the family, particularly critical during periods of transition, such as moving to sixth form, college, university and employment. I've also thought about a simple screening process for all referrals, regardless of the reason, in order to prevent children from being missed on multiple occasions, whilst not diagnostic it could highlight if there was potential ASC at an early stage and then give parents the opportunity to explore it further for themselves under the guidance of CAMHS. It would have been helpful for us if ASC had been suggested at any stage prior to my epiphany, because, if I had known about it, I could have researched it and found the tick list online and saved precious years of trying to make a square peg of a child fit into a round hole. This could be achieved by a series of simple questions using an emotional rating scale using emoji-type faces giving the opportunity to see whether they can recognise expressions as well as the tell-tale answers to questions/statements themselves being geared towards typical ASC behaviour, e.g. 'How do you feel when people stand very close to you/unfamiliar adults talk to you/you don't have friends to play with?', followed by a series of facial expressions including the obvious ones and then more complex subtle ones. Talking about how the children perceive/interpret the emojis themselves could be enlightening enough?

Darcey: I was lucky to have access to Fiona and the help that I got, but now there isn't really very much. People with ASC are finding it difficult to get diagnosed or finding it hard even to find services to go to. There should also be services available for people who have siblings with ASC, because they have to live with the effects of it too, and despite Freya having known and seen me at home since I was diagnosed, which was a very long time ago, she still struggles to cope now and still finds it hard. It shouldn't be difficult for someone with ASC or even people who think they might have it to get the help they need. Currently it's a struggle, and I'm very lucky to have been diagnosed in a process of several years ago, which is quite a lot. Other conditions such as dyslexia are very accessible for diagnosis and well known, but Asperger's is so well known now and getting more common, e.g. 1:100, and there's still very limited services, which I find shocking. But not only that, hardly anyone really seems to understand or know what ASC actually is. People should be made more aware of it, but accurately, especially mentioning that boys and girls are different when it comes to ASC. It is made known now, but some of it is wrong in my opinion, and I don't seem to be able to find information on what I personally go through, making me and possibly other girls feel we're on our own. Friends around me who know I have it still can't get to grips with the fact that I have it, because all the stereotyped information trying to make people understand and aware doesn't apply to every girl with ASC. Personally, I'm unsure as to whether it should be taught in school, as I used to find it embarrassing when they would say things that were untrue about it. But schools should definitely be made aware of it and, once the understanding is more accurate, then maybe I think it should be taught. Other conditions are not as vague and are more understood so ASC should be too. Because I have missed out on many opportunities to help my education because no one knew at the time or I never brought it up when teachers would do things that affect my ability to learn (accidentally), because they didn't know. But services should definitely be more available for people to be diagnosed or helped.

CONTINUED PROVISION

Like the rest of the pathways currently in place for assessment, diagnosis and therapies, this is inconsistent and ages for transition vary, and processes and systems vary as do eligibility criteria.

Clinicians, we need to think out of the box.

Be brave. Stretch yourselves. Be hungry to learn. Look at yourselves and develop yourselves, as we are expecting our young women to. Be flexible in your beliefs and models of working. Your flexibility will allow you into your young person's mind. You need to reach in to them. Don't expect them to be able to come to you in the early days of a therapeutic relationship. Work hard and you will reap the benefits. Work through your frustrations, as these are not quick fixes; you are in it for the long haul and so you should be.

Time, energy, compassion and patience are what is needed. As long as you are moving in the right direction, keep going and, if you're not, find another way. As you can see from the three remarkable young women in this book, invest in them and they will reward you with their excellence and brilliance and wellness. As a clinician what more would you need than that? That is your reward. That is your energy and motivation to keep going.

The service needs to allow clinicians to adapt and enhance their practice and allow clinical exposure to difference, regular reflection and checking their practice. Appointments need to lend themselves to you being able to communicate with your children, young people and their families and to allow time and opportunities to watch and learn from your colleagues, read and observe. I found that my experience, humanity, humility and respect for the individuals with whom I work and my profession motivated me to deliver an individualised way of working.

Being different is not wrong; being different should be embraced and therefore services should be different and managers and commissioners should work with those you want to develop these kinds of services.

Reassuring and being kind to your young people, their families and your colleagues is vital. Take care of each other. We sometimes get this right with our clients, but not so much with our colleagues. We get so stressed and restricted with our time and as our own emotional wells are often running on low we don't have the physical or emotional time for others.

Working within CAMHS means you are often greeted wherever you go with negativity, especially from other services and from families who have had challenging experiences with us as a service. Your colleagues are experiencing the same frustrations within services that you are, so it can be difficult to have time and space to look after each other. Ironically, we are the worst at this, and yet we are working within a mental health service. Management and commissioning need to ensure their teams have time to breathe. We can't offer the quality timely services if we are at our own low ebb. We too are human and have families and lives, and we need to be able to go home and put energy into those places, as these are the people who more often than not make sure we are OK to come back to work each day, in addition to our own selves who, if able to recharge at home, can support our families much better.

Careful establishment of trust is extremely important. I can't emphasis this enough. This has to be from an organisation standpoint and from an individual perspective. We need to remember that the young people we work with have difficulties with social communication and interactions so we need to ensure our services accommodate and adapt to this. Trust is crucial. Being full of candour and openness, being honest and truthful are imperative. Patience, empathy and insight are essentials. You will need to be intelligent, as these young women will stretch your knowledge and your intelligence. You will need not only to be intelligent, but you will need to think smart. You will need to be able to compensate for communication difficulties with other knowledge and skills.

As service providers we need to ensure that these young women are no longer invisible to our services, that they are not overlooked or discounted. We need to use different ways of communicating our young people's difficulties to them and others. For example, we should not describe their autism as mild. This is hugely misleading. If they succeed at school and do extracurricular activities, it can be misunderstood, as they may be and often are masking considerable underlying issues. They are often engaged in compensatory learning whilst experiencing severe generalised and social anxiety. They are often in a constant state of confusion and distress, which eventually manifests itself in major panic attacks or 'meltdowns' and sometimes even in a way as concerning and debilitating as a psychotic episode. Early recognition of social communication difficulties and anxiety can avoid all of this.

Regular, appropriate training and research gathering needs to be more encouraged and embedded within your continuing professional development (CPD), so clinical and management supervisors need to support you in your requests for conferences, engaging in research, or secondments into other services, as conditions like OCD or ADHD, which can be standalone conditions, can be overlooked and just accepted in isolation, often seen in young women who bounce in and out of services. Anorexia could be unusual eating behaviour. Emotional dysregulation cycles can be seen as bipolar. Descriptions of perception, fantasy novel-like language and running thoughts or conversations out loud can be mistaken for psychosis. Oppositional defiant behaviour can be a manifestation of an autistic child's difficulties with theory of mind and emotional dysregulation rather than purely behaviour. Anxiety and depression may be due to an undiagnosed ASC. An episodic psychosis may be underlying ASC not psychosis. ASC can mimic many psychiatric disorders but can also be intertwined and/or running alongside.

Special interests differ. They are often less obvious, less likely to be imposed on others. Girls with ASC tend to show difficulties when interacting with females with those social subtleties and often can be misunderstood as unladylike rather than sociably inept. They can adopt other personas, which puts them at risk of remaining forever undiagnosed, marginalised and continually puzzled about the complexities of the social world. Due to their ability to blend in and mimic eye contact and sometimes whole personalities, schools often miss their difficulties as they never see the true person behind the masking.

The argument of labels continues within the clinical field, within families and for individuals themselves. We need to be mindful as a service that we keep a balanced opinion and advise accordingly, void of our personal opinion. I like to explain it in the context of the differences the young people feel have a name in this context, but we are all different and have differences. It's just that most of our differences don't have a name. If you think from a positive stance, it can assist with self-understanding and self-identity. This can end up with denial of resources, and the understanding that it is a cognitive difficulty rather than a moral deviance can be helpful, as it opens up how to make sense of yourself, resulting in you being able succeed at what you are. Looked at from a negative stance, it can become a burden and seen as something that stops you doing things. Currently the only limitation is in joining one of the armed forces, but that is also being considered carefully.

Having no follow-up to diagnosis is disastrous and sometimes catastrophic; we wouldn't diagnose other significant conditions and offer no follow-up or understanding of the condition.

A hot potato at the moment is the issue of gender identity and, with the rate of referrals increasing and the age of referrals becoming much wider, we as a service and profession need to be clear in our pathways and delivery of those pathways. As clinicians we need to be informed enough to offer support appropriately in the form of treatment, referrals and signposting. I do feel that with the young people I work with, who are querying their difficulties within the social communication arena or who have already got a diagnosis, an ungendered or gender confused identity issue lies in addressing autistic versus neurotypical identity rather than gender identity or sexual orientation. The young person therefore gets to know who they are before they decide what gender they feel most comfortable being.

Interventions and therapies need to embrace the unique clinical presentation and adapt autism-friendly approaches. But professional bodies need to consider extensive research in all clinical areas before making particular therapies into rigid pathways and investing into how disciplines are trained and to what standard in the understanding of ASC. I have found cognitive/psychometric testing invaluable to inform therapy, as uneven profiles may result in advice being offered beyond the individual's capability without sufficient detail or information or without being delivered in a way that is understandable and meaningful to them. Specific testing like memory and executive dysfunction testing is particularly helpful in ASC. This requires skilled trained psychologists to complete the assessments and full Weschler Intelligence Scales for children can be very time consuming. More understanding for clinicians and what is most helpful to ask for, and more training for psychologists to be able to perform the assessment are advisable. Proceed with caution, however, as a lot of these tests are very rigid in the way they have to be delivered, sometimes causing difficulties for different thinking brains. Having a team of psychologists in CAMHS is essential and very much valued by other members of the team. It scaffolds the other work which goes alongside.

There has been a shift to involve service users much more in the say of how services should be run and this is a theme that is currently very apparent. This is only helpful, however, if the information collected is used and distributed to the right people in the right places. What often happens is that there is a change in government, or targets and objectives and finances change, and the information is either not used or used in a way that is unrecognisable and not able to be implemented in the current system.

The current driver from the government is to have CAMHS more accessible in schools. I have been involved in this, and it definitely means you can reach a larger population more quickly and in a more reactive manner. Referrals can be made directly to allied professionals and children identified as needing CAMHS input get referred straight in, bypassing their GP and waiting times. It improves interagency working and understanding and pools resources, knowledge and expertise. From that grows clinical respect, and this in turn benefits the young person as the service is more wraparound, appropriate, timely and streamlined.

Supervision is vital not only for professional development but for ensuring support and guidance are regular and appropriate. We work with young people with significant complexities and what comes with that is a need to have peer, individual clinical and management supervision. This ensures safe and effective practice, which ensures an excellent quality service. It encourages clinicians to know their own personal and professional limitations and to be able to ask for help and support.

Planning for transitions needs to start early and not only be a consideration for junior to secondary but home to nursery, infant to juniors, high school to college and then into adult services.

Careful planning, seamless communication and joint working are crucial.

Conclusion

Misdiagnosis and misunderstanding of girls/young women within the autism arena need to be addressed, as they deserve and are entitled to an increase not only in clinical understanding, knowledge and skill but in resources and quality, timely assessments and appropriate therapy and treatment at every stage of their lives. The consequence of not doing this, as we have seen from some of the information shared in the previous chapters, will be a detrimental impact on individuals' emotional and physical wellbeing, which can be and has been catastrophic.

There is also the impact on our community, not only in terms of the contributions these young women can make to their community, but also in terms of the cost on services, which can be extensive. There will be an increase in the prescribing of medications and inpatient admissions will increase. Currently, appropriate services for individuals with ASC and additional mental health needs are scarce. Re-referrals into services are increasing and, unless drastic action is taken, individuals will continue to revolve in and out, not being able to access appropriate services for their need.

These young women will often not be able to access education due to their anxiety, which in turn results in their emotional wellbeing being impacted even more, and so the rotation continues. Some girls and young women are out of school for considerable amounts of time and sometimes end up in inappropriate educational and residential settings, adding to their anxiety and increasing negative belief cycles about themselves. Learning is stunted and halted and mental health and behavioural difficulties become more significant.

It is important to remember to include and involve the girls' families, unless there is good reason not to. Parents, grandparents, carers and siblings, whoever is important to your young person, cats, dogs – use them.

If your young women are in the care system, make sure you communicate with your colleagues from different teams. Work collaboratively and with respect. Keep sight of your goal for your young woman. Involve her. Demonstrate the collaborative working to her, ensure excellent safeguarding and management systems wrap around your young person ensuring these are implemented and support and encourage good parenting within the care staff team. Don't be afraid to challenge, but do it constructively alongside your colleagues.

I feel I need to acknowledge those girls and young women (of whom I have known many, too many) who do not have the supportive networks of their families or have parents that are unwell and not able to fight for their children, or parents who are too exhausted or lacking in confidence to take on these huge establishments to get what they need for their children. We should not live in a society that needs you to complain to get a quality service for your child, and we should definitely not be only responding to those who are able to articulate and communicate their distress or concerns above other young people and their families for more timely or more quality services. Services should be in place so people are not backed into a corner to have to come out fighting for their children and so other less determined families are left with a lesser service.

Remember your young women. Don't lose sight of them as being just them. Find out about them. What makes them who they are? What are their interests, motivators? Learn about the things they like. Share their interests. You never know: you might learn something or find a new passion yourself.

Keep yourselves up to date in your clinical practice, challenge your services to ensure you are given opportunities to learn and grow to develop your clinical skills.

Don't collude with short cuts to put plasters over under-resourced services; speak up, use your knowledge and expertise to ensure quality care is delivered to this particular group of young people.

Remember to role model behaviour, be honest, be firm but fair, be flexible in your practice but, most importantly, enjoy your time with them, enjoy their difference, learn from their difference, celebrate and encourage their difference; you are in control of that. By doing so you will gain trust and mutual respect will grow and you will experience enriching relationships which help you, too, to grow in your work and enhance who you are as a person.

Do not give up. I still come across clinicians who don't believe me when I offer my evidence and rationale for my formulation of difficulties observed and evidenced.

And, if you don't know or are unsure, don't rush; keep looking until you can ensure you are signposting appropriately.

Thankfully Milly, Esther and Darcey did eventually receive services and diagnosis that have been helpful to them, but this required a joint effort from all involved, working together with the same aim and the same conviction. Every piece of that jigsaw is required to enable that young person to get to the place of resilience and emotional and physical wellbeing they need to be to be the best they can be.

MILLY, DARCEY AND ESTHER NOW

Milly, 2017: Over the past few years I have done things I never could have seen myself doing when I was younger. When I was 16 I couldn't even go to the post office because I was worried I wouldn't know what to say or do, but by the time I was 18 I managed to live away from home whilst I went to university, and even get a part time job. I also succeeded in passing my driving test after a long and difficult journey. I am now living independently and in full time employment, and on a part time college course through my work, which will help me to forge a career in accountancy.

Darcey, 2017: I plan to go to university to study psychology. I have always been interested in that area ever since my diagnosis and I find the subject interesting too. As a career, I'm still unknown. I want to travel and maybe go into being a clinical psychologist.

Having Asperger's means it's a lot harder for me to step out of my comfort zone. I love adventure and travelling so any challenge related to it I get myself involved in. Though I try and back out at the last-minute due to anxiety and fear I end up enjoying it usually. I have NCS, Duke of Edinburgh and am about to go on a World Challenge to Tanzania. I've learnt to communicate a lot better by working at dancing. I found it difficult at first, to deal with random situations and talking to parents or entertaining the kids, but now I feel I am great at it and it's helped me cope with spontaneous situations or communicating with strangers.

Darcey is now at university studying psychology, living in student accommodation and she completed and enjoyed her challenge in Tanzania.

Esther: What do I have planned for the future?

World domination. But until my death ray starts working, I'm planning to do something that includes graphics and computers. My list is currently at web page design or ux design. I can also do like acting as I am quite dramatic on stage. Off-stage I stare into your soul and devour it. When I actually make eye contact, of course.

My achievements: I once ruled Albion (Xbox game, Fable 3) but my save was lost. I also got good grades on my SATs (statutory assessments carried out in primary schools in England) and I'm currently at target Grade 5 and 6 for most subjects (I can follow the teacher's instructions unlike some people). I couldn't manage doing the practicals for food tech last year but this year I got an extended on my shortbread. It certainly helps I no longer have idiots running around *my* kitchen. In Year 7 (ages 11–12) I left the United Kingdom for the first time and set foot in France. It was only a two-day trip because my sheer amazing perfectness was needed in the classroom. The first time I left my parents lonely and afraid, them not me, was in Year 6 (ages 10–11) when I went away on a two- to four-day trip. The fire alarm appreciated me so much it woke me up three times on the last night to say how sad it was that I was leaving.

All these young women continue to have difficult times in their lives. What they now have though is an understanding and acceptance of themselves and ways of managing their individual difficulties.

They did this with help and support from people who valued, encouraged, supported, liked, loved and accepted them for being themselves. They did this with professionals who liked, respected and supported their growth and understanding of themselves. They did this with their own bravery, their determination, their motivation and by using their differences in a positive way.

Some words from some other truly inspiring women:

Alix Generous, a young woman with Asperger's, a mental health advocate, author, speaker and scientist wrote:

> This world is in desperate need of creative and intellectual minds to solve complex problems. But before we can do that, we need to build a culture that accepts mental diversity. (Generous n.d.)

> For the love of Ann, they struggled to give her a life and the ability to find herself and the world and all its beauty. They succeeded against all the odds. (Copeland and Hodges 1976, p.153)

> I am different...not less. (Temple Grandin, in Grandin and Attwood 2012)

Some final words from me:

> Be the best clinician and person you can be, fight for the best services for your young women as it's time to embrace, encourage and promote difference and uniqueness.

Then hopefully these young women will be:

> Miss Understood.

References

American Psychiatric Association (2013) *Diagnostic and Statistical Manual of Mental Disorders*, 5th edition. Washington, DC: American Psychiatric Associaton Publishing.

Arnold, C. (2016) 'The *invisible link* between autism and anorexia.' *Spectrum*, 17 February. Accessed on 15/02/2018 at https://spectrumnews.org/features/deep-dive/the-invisible-link-between-autism-and-anorexia

Attwood, T., Garnett, M. and Rynkiewicz, A. (2016) 'Q-ASC Questionnaire for Autism Spectrum Conditions age 5–19.' Accessed on 15/02/2018 at http://spectrumascmed.com/wp-content/uploads/2016/08/Fragment-Q-ASC.pdf

Baron-Cohen, S. (2008) *Autism and Asperger Syndrome: The Facts.* Oxford: Oxford University Press.

Baron-Cohen, S., Johnson, D., Asher, J., Wheelwright, S. *et al.* (2013) 'Is synaesthesia more common in autism?' *Molecular Autism 4*, 1, 40. Accessed on 30/01/2018 at http://dx.doi.org/10.1186/2040-2392-4-40

Chawarska, K., Klin, A. and Volkmar, F. (2008) *Autism Spectrum Disorders in Infants and Toddlers.* New York: Guilford Press.

Colombi, C. and Ghaziuddin, M. (2017) 'Neuropsychological characteristics of children with mixed autism and ADHD.' *Autism Research and Treatment 2017*, 1–5. Accessed on 30/01/2018 at http://dx.doi.org/10.1155/2017/5781781

Copeland, J. and Hodges, J. (1976) *For the Love of Ann.* London: Arrow Books.

Duerden, E., Oatley, H., Mak-Fan, K., McGrath, P. *et al.* (2012) 'Risk factors associated with self-injurious behaviors in children and adolescents with autism spectrum disorders.' *Journal of Autism and Developmental Disorders 42*, 11, 2460–2470. Accessed on 30/01/2018 at http://dx.doi.org/10.1007/s10803-012-1497-9

Generous, A. (n.d.) Home page. Accessed on 15/02/2018 at www.alixgenerous.com

Giarelli, E., Wiggins, L., Rice, C., Levy, S. *et al.* (2010) 'Sex differences in the evaluation and diagnosis of autism spectrum disorders among children.' *Disability and Health Journal 3*, 2, 107–116. Accessed on 30/01/2018 at http://dx.doi.org/10.1016/j.dhjo.2009.07.001

Grandin, T. and Attwood, T. (2012) *Different...Not Less.* Arlington, TX: Future Horizons.

Hendrickx, S. (2015) *Women and Girls with Autism Spectrum Disorder.* London: Jessica Kingsley Publishers.

H M Government (2009) Autism Act 2009. Norwich: Stationery Office. Accessed on 13/12/2017 at www.legislation.gov.uk/ukpga/2009/15/contents

Irlen (2017) 'Irlen.' Accessed on 30/01/2018 at www.irlen.com

Lai, M., Lombardo, M., Pasco, G., Ruigrok, A. *et al.* (2011) 'A behavioral comparison of male and female adults with high functioning autism spectrum conditions.' *PLoS ONE 6*, 6. Accessed on 30/01/2018 at http://dx.doi.org/10.1371/journal.pone.0020835

Montague, R. and Rastall, E. (2013) 'The Autism Blog.' Seattle Children's Hospital Research Foundation. Obsessive Compulsive Disorder and Autism Spectrum Disorder, October 11.

NICE (2017) 'The National Institute for Health and Care Excellence.' Accessed on 30/01/2018 at www.nice.org.uk/guidance/cg28

Pinto, T. (2017) 'Girls with autism are getting a rougher deal than boys because our assessments are so male orientated.' *The Independent*, 21 August.

Simeon, D. and Favazza, A.R. (2001) 'Self-Injurious Behaviors: Phenomenology and Assessment.' In D. Simeon and E. Hollander (eds.) *Self-Injurious Behaviors: Assessment and Treatment.* Washington, DC: American Psychiatric Association Publishing.

Simone, R. (2010) *Aspergirls.* London: Jessica Kingsley Publishers.

Supekar, K. and Menon, V. (2015) 'Sex differences in structural organization of motor systems and their dissociable links with repetitive/restricted behaviors in children with autism.' *Molecular Autism 6*, 50.

Werling, D. and Geschwind, D. (2013) 'Sex differences in autism spectrum disorders.' *Current Opinion in Neurology 26*, 2, 146–153. Accessed on 30/01/2018 at http://dx.doi.org/10.1097/wco.0b013e32835ee548

Yaull-Smith, D. (2008) 'Gender and Autism.' *Autism Hampshire.* Accessed on 30/01/2018 at https://www.autismhampshire.org.uk/about-autism/gender-and-autism.html

Index